Praise for *Surviving Domestic Violence*

"The book is friendly, compassionate, and understanding. The exercises are right on point, systematic, and practical. You have dived in deeply to the different internal realities that a woman goes through when facing intimate oppression, breaking them down so concretely and specifically that she will keep saying, 'Oh, yes, oh, yes' as she reads it. No existing book creates this kind of detailed, reality-based, and workable plan for healing and action. Perhaps most important, this will actually work for people, which is of course what matters the most. This book is clearly going to be one of the most valuable pieces ever written about domestic violence."

—Lundy Bancroft, author of *Why Does He Do That: Inside the Minds of Angry and Controlling Men*, and *Should I Stay or Should I Go? A Guide to Knowing If Your Relationship Can—and Should—Be Saved*

"This work is what has been missing in our society's response to domestic violence! It provides practical guidelines for a journey of identification as Victim to Survivor to a new identity as a Thriver. It offers practical guidelines for crafting life rituals to mark important passages. This work will help generations of women avoid lives defined by trauma and abuse. Highly recommended as required reading for those willing to reshape their life stories—especially if searching to lead lives radically different from those modeled to accept abuse as normal."

—Kathleen Carrick, PhD, MSW, editor and author of *Domestic Violence in Rural Underserved Areas: A Guide to Working with Diverse Communities*

D0753845

Praise for *Surviving Domestic Violence*

"Impressive."

> —W. Penn Handwerker, author of *Women's Power and Social Revolution: Fertility Transition in the West Indies*, *The Origin of Cultures*, and *Quick Ethnography*

"*Surviving Domestic Violence* offers steps to take to make your life as fulfilling and joyful as possible."

> —Patricia Evans, author of *The Verbally Abusive Relationship*

Surviving Domestic Violence

—— A Guide to ——
Healing Your Soul and
Building Your Future

Danielle F. Wozniak, MSW, ACSW, PhD
and Karen Allen, MSW, LCSW, PhD

Avon, Massachusetts

Published by
Adams Media, a division of F+W Media, Inc.
57 Littlefield Street, Avon, MA 02322. U.S.A.
www.adamsmedia.com

ISBN 10: 1-4405-4271-6
ISBN 13: 978-1-4405-4271-8
eISBN 10: 1-4405-4293-7
eISBN 13: 978-1-4405-4293-0

Printed in the United States of America.

10   9   8   7   6   5   4   3   2   1

This publication is designed to provide accurate and authoritative information with regard to the subject matter covered. It is sold with the understanding that the publisher is not engaged in rendering legal, accounting, or other professional advice. If legal advice or other expert assistance is required, the services of a competent professional person should be sought.

—From a *Declaration of Principles* jointly adopted by a Committee of the American Bar Association and a Committee of Publishers and Associations

Many of the designations used by manufacturers and sellers to distinguish their product are claimed as trademarks. Where those designations appear in this book and F+W Media was aware of a trademark claim, the designations have been printed with initial capital letters.

This book is available at quantity discounts for bulk purchases.
For information, please call 1-800-289-0963.

Contents

This book is dedicated to those whose love, support, and joy allowed us to traverse our own healing journeys and be a light for other women.

For Jeff, Eliana, and Solomon, who inspire, support, and sustain me and who remind me daily what joy is and how empty life would be without it. —Danielle

For Jim Allen, whose gentleness, wisdom, and patience is a constant source of inspiration to me. —With love, Karen

Acknowledgments

First and foremost, we wish to acknowledge all of the women who participated in the shaping and refining of this work. As women participated in our groups they suggested new activities and helped us refine existing ones. And thus our work for the last seven years has been fluid, organic, and shaped by participants. They also shared their most tender and valiant struggles to reclaim themselves and allowed us to accompany them on the journey. For that we are deeply honored and grateful.

We also offer our gratitude to women who worked as research assistants and graduate students who tirelessly coded data, reviewed research, wrote meditations, and further developed exercises. We would especially like to thank Robin Gregory, who contributed brilliant ideas and content to this book; Amy Kalil; Amanda Stovall; and Darcy Sant. We would like to thank Kate Pruitt-Chapin and Tammy Tolleson Knee; Eilis O'Herrily; Susie DeVietro; and Adrienne Gasperoni, who ran groups in various stages of our group development.

And we would like to thank the bevvy of scholars, writers, activists, and healers who shared with us their wisdom, insight, critiques, and support. It is a long list and we are bound to leave someone out, only to remember him or her after the book is printed. Please know that we are very grateful for your contributions. Here is the start of our list:

We wish to thank W. Penn Handwerker who consistently believed in this work, saw its importance, and kept urging us onward. We want to thank Marlene Hutchins, friend, neighbor and coder extraordinaire who helped this book come into clear focus as she developed graphics and coded text and talked about content. We thank the mothers who forged the path in this kind of work—Susan Omilian, who was a pioneer in Thriving work as a part of a larger sequence in healing; as was Sharon Maynard, who implemented healing work through the Mohegan Tribal Elders; and Barbara Whitfield Harris (*www.barbarawhitfield.com*), whose extensive work on Thriving and spirituality was critical to our thinking. We want to thank Trudy Griswold (*www.angelspeake.com*), whose knowledge and ability to teach others about angels have been a real—well, Godsend. And finally, we want to thank folks like Alan Rosenspan, whose article, "How to Be Insanely Creative," kept us thinking about the elements of creativity as critical components of healing; Melissa Bradley Bell, whose healing workshops were invaluable; Kevin Kinchen, creator of the Power of Thought Newsletter (*www.creativepowerofthought.com*), from whom we drew spiritual inspiration; and Bill Grace, founder of Common Good, a nonprofit organization dedicated to "Inspiring Courage, Hope and Action for Just Communities," who helped us think about core values; and the multitude of folks from whom we gathered perspectives on backward goal setting as a means to achieving perfection.

We finally want to thank Lundy Bancroft, whose tireless research and educational efforts shed critical light on our understanding of batterers and whose brilliance made this book shine brighter. Thank you.

Introduction

Welcome to Your Healing Journey

> **This book is meant for women who have left their abusive situation. If you are not yet in a safe place, STOP! Connect with your local women's shelter immediately for help.**

Sadly, the vocabulary has become all too commonplace these days. Words like "abuse" and "domestic violence" typically describe physical abuse that occurs in a marriage or an intimate relationship. But there are many types of violating relationships and many types of violations. Perhaps you were violated as a child, either through sexual, physical, or verbal abuse or by helplessly watching your mother or siblings being abused. Perhaps you were violated in adulthood through a partner who verbally or physically or emotionally hurt, controlled, or degraded you. Or perhaps you have been violated, bullied, or harassed by coworkers or bosses while on the job.

Regardless of how you arrived here, you are forever changed by your experiences. Yet these violations do not have to define who you are. This book offers you the opportunity to embark on a healing journey that will bring you to a new place of self-awareness and happiness. You'll be able to place the violation you experienced in a context such that it does not dominate who you are now.

This workbook will guide you through the transitions necessary to turn your experiences with violation into the kind of transformation that cannot just improve your life, but can actually help you create your ideal life. Does this sound amazing? Does it sound scary? Does it sound too good to be true, or too much to hope for? It isn't. We will help you remember how to hope, we will coach you in how to dream, and we will teach you how to ask for what you want. Our motto is: If you can dream it, you can see it. If you can see it, you can get there.

To find your ideal life, you do not need to depend on anyone but yourself. You have probably discovered that Prince Charming does not really exist. This book is not about a rescue that won't happen—you don't need it anyway, believe it or not. Yes, having people support you is important and helpful. But the truth is, you already possess all the power you need. Like Dorothy in *The Wizard of Oz,* you will learn that you have the power to change your life; you have the power to create everything you could possibly want. You have always had it. This power allowed you to survive violation and it's the same power you tapped into in order to leave a violating relationship. It is this strength and power that you will expand as you take steps toward healing.

Perhaps one of the most important things to consider now is this: If you are feeling scared or empty or uncertain or confused, know that you won't always feel the way you do now. You will get through this period in your life. You can emerge on the other side of it feeling very good about who you are and where you are going. Rebuilding is hard work. But you are worth it!

This book is written for women who have taken the same first steps as you have, by women who will guide you through what lies ahead: healing, change, a new way of looking at yourself, and new life possibilities. You weren't alone when you were being victimized, even though it might have felt like it. You're not alone now as you struggle to survive and put one foot in front of the other to create a new life. And you will not be alone as you take your next steps toward healing and thriving. You are part of a community of survivors, many of whom become women who use their experiences as victims and survivors to thrive, both in spite of and because of their experiences.

A Word about the Authors

The women behind the words in this book are Danielle F. Wozniak and Karen Allen. Both of us are clinical social workers, professors, and hold positions of leadership at our institutions. Yet both of us have also experienced violating relationships and traumas in our past. We had to come to terms with the abuse and undertake our own healing journeys. Our professional and personal experiences motivated us to help other women who have suffered in violating relationships, and this led to creating activity-based support groups that Danielle christened "Rites of Passage Groups." We have facilitated these groups and witnessed the powerful transformations that take place when women are able to really let go of blaming themselves for the past and begin to actively create a safe and promising future for themselves. When we saw how effective and helpful the groups were we decided to write this book so that every woman who wanted to heal could have that opportunity.

How to Use This Book

Healing from any wound happens gradually and in a certain sequence. Your emotional healing from violation is no different. You might already be talking to a therapist or trained professional to work through your experience. You can still benefit from this book—individual or group therapy and this book are not mutually exclusive. No matter where you are on your road to recovery, you'll find some important pieces of information in this book that can help you feel better. Shortly after leaving a violating relationship, Danielle went back to school. She was new on campus and was lost most of the time. A woman in admissions directed her to a building and then asked, "Honey, do you know where you are going?" This question was piercing because it touched the truth. She didn't know where she was going and just had to hope that the direction she had chosen for her life was the right one. Like Danielle's experiences, some of your journey will be by trial and error and some will be part of a very intentional change process. This book will help you reduce the scared and confusing feelings that can come with any new life navigation, help you reduce the trial-and-error period, and offer you the road map we all need during difficult and confusing times of life change.

One of the most important ways to heal from violence and initiate such a life change is by shifting your thinking about yourself, about what you want out of life, and about what relationships are and should be. To start, we'll talk briefly about what you have been through, because that's an important part of letting go and healing from trauma. Then, we'll move on to talking about your future, because that's an important part of rebuilding and creating your new life.

This book is organized into units. Each unit offers you information about the phase you're currently in, and an array of opportunities to fully explore and develop the new skills outlined in the beginning of each unit. Each skill is meant to be learned sequentially and built upon to best navigate your healing journey. The interactive activities you'll find throughout each unit are designed to help you shift your thinking so that you can begin to make changes in your life. You can jot notes in the margins of this book, but a better idea is to get a notebook or journal where you can write your answers to the exercises and track your feelings as you progress on your healing journey. This journal will not only provide a space for you to write; it will represent a scrapbook of how far you've come.

Research has shown that there is a connection between your thoughts and the reality you create based on those thoughts. So in order to change your life, you must change the way you think about your life. You must think new thoughts based on new possibilities and new ideas, and then put those thoughts into action. This takes practice, and begins with "baby steps." Some of the activities to help you make these baby steps are simple for this very reason. The bits of progress you make today set the stage for the big changes you'll see down the road. These changes also involve using a tool you may have not used for a while: your imagination. Some activities will be more helpful to you than others, and you will enjoy some more than others. Still, we encourage you to give them all a try and see what feels right and seems to fit with your current needs. Take your time, try to enjoy doing the activities, and enjoy the journey they take you on. Keep this book handy for the future, too. Some activities that don't fit well with your journey today may be a perfect fit later. You may want to revisit activities over time.

Your journey out of your painful past and into your bright, happy future begins now. Take a deep breath, turn the page, and get started!

A Last Look Back: Understanding Abuse

"Faith is taking the first step even when you don't see the whole staircase."
—MARTIN LUTHER KING JR.

In this unit, you will:

- Understand some of the dynamics of abuse
- Explore the impact abuse has had on you
- Learn about current feelings you might be experiencing

The First Step

This unit is called "A Last Look Back" because when you have left a violating relationship, it is important to tell your story, and to process your experiences with violation with a trained professional or in a support group. It is also important to understand some of the dynamics of abuse. While the majority of this book will help you look *ahead* and actively create a life without violation, in this chapter, we want to briefly look *back* in order to:

- Point out some common themes, experiences, and feelings that women share who have been in violating relationships.
- Give you a chance to get some of those concerns and feelings out in plain sight, where you can begin to work through them.
- Let you know that where you are now is perfectly normal.
- Show you how to move ahead.

If you have left an abusive relationship, you have already done the hardest part. It may not feel that way at this early stage, but you've done something very brave and life-changing. You have gotten yourself to a place where you are not being abused or violated and can begin to taste what it feels like to be safe. By stopping the abuse, you launched a journey to reclaim your personal power, to become who you want to be, and to heal from the violation you have experienced.

Terminology

Before we get started, let's take a look at some of the terms you'll see frequently throughout this book.

Gender

As a "default," we'll use the pronoun "she"/"her" for the victim of the violation, and "he" for the perpetrator. That's because in the vast majority of cases, men abuse women. If that's not the case for you, simply change the pronouns to match your situation.

Violation vs. Violence

In this book, we use the term *violation* rather than *violence* because violation refers to what happened to you inside. It describes the feelings of being wounded, hurt, or traumatized, whether physically or emotionally. It focuses on you, rather than referring to the behavior of the person who caused the wounds. In other words, the word "violation" keeps the spotlight on you and validates your feelings. It emphasizes your experiences and even tells what lies ahead for you—the necessity for healing.

Learning about Abuse

As you deal with the aftermath of abuse, it is important to understand that you are not alone. Domestic violence occurs in every socioeconomic class, culture, and community in the United States. In fact, according to the Centers for Disease Control and Prevention, more than half of all women experience an abusive relationship in their lifetime and one-quarter of all women are raped by the time they are twenty-five.

What Is Abuse?

Beverly Engel, author of *The Emotionally Abused Woman*, defines abuse as "any behavior that is designed to control and subjugate another human being through the use of fear, humiliation, and verbal or physical assaults." The use of fear, threats, and humiliation are enough to constitute violating behavior; it is not necessary for an actual physical assault to happen for a relationship to be abusive.

Abusers work by isolating a woman from her friends, her family, and often her own children. And they work by isolating women from themselves. Before long, you are in a relationship cut off from everyone and you have no support. You also begin to lose a sense of who you are as a real and whole individual. Instead, you come to see yourself only as a piece of, or an extension of, your abuser. (No wonder it is so hard to leave—this type of erosion makes it very hard to ever think you can leave or survive without him.)

Excessive jealousy is also a common feature. In the beginning stages of a relationship, a woman may be flattered that her partner thinks that she is desirable to others. The jealousy soon escalates and intensifies, however, and may involve stalking and spying on a woman. Coercing a woman to have sex when it is unwanted, even within a relationship, is a form of rape and violation. Physical assault, which includes hitting, pushing, shoving, choking, and throwing objects, also constitutes abuse.

The Cycle of Abusive Relationships

Lenore E. Walker, author of *The Battered Woman*, identified a cycle that was typical of abusive relationships. She called this the "cycle of violence," which consists of three phases:

1. The first stage is called **tension building** and occurs when anger and tension start to build. Women tell us that at times they provoked their partners into explosive behavior during the tension-building phase because the anxiety of not knowing when the blowup was going to occur was so uncomfortable. Knowing the abuse was coming, they wanted to get it over with. One woman told us that by provoking her partner, she at least had some control over when and where the abuse would happen.
2. The second phase is the **abusive or acute phase** and involves major outbursts of anger, threats, name-calling, and assault.
3. Following this a **honeymoon phase** may occur, in which the abuser expresses regret, is fearful of losing the woman, and makes apologetic gestures.

The "honeymoon" phase can have a powerful effect on preventing a woman from leaving, and can also be what women focus on when they are second-guessing themselves after they have left. In fact, the loss of affection and closeness that you felt during honeymoon phases is a legitimate loss, and like all losses, it has to be mourned. Yet, keep in mind that you can and will have that intimacy in a relationship in the future—but without the abuse and violence surrounding it.

What Is Emotional Abuse?

Wounds from emotional and psychological abuse are not as visible as bruises or broken bones. However, research has shown that this type of violence may in fact be more damaging than other types of abuse. In the journal *Violence and Victims*, Richard Tolman, MSW, PhD, identified two dominant kinds of psychological abuse that occur in violating relationships:

1. **Dominance-isolation**, which involves isolation, financial control, using words or actions that are degrading, holding rigid ideas about male and female roles, and withholding emotional support.
2. **Emotional-verbal**, in which the abuser demands that he be the center of the woman's world and attention at all times and psychologically manipulates the woman until she feels as if she is losing her sanity. Name-calling and telling the woman she is worthless or would be "nothing" without her abusive partner are examples of the kind of degradation tactics abusive men use.

It is not at all uncommon for both types of psychological abuse to be part of an abusive relationship.

Leaving behind these types of abusive situations can be more difficult because there seems to be no visible harm and if family or friends haven't heard this kind of abuse from your partner, they may not even realize that it has been going on. If your partner was charming in public, they may also struggle to believe you. This may intensify your questioning about whether this was really abuse or not. You may feel like you are crazy or that this wasn't as bad as you thought, or that maybe it was in your head. If you're feeling this way, consider this:

Every person deserves the resources and support to realize her full potential. A relationship in which there is emotional and psychological abuse stunts or prevents you from personally growing and leading a fulfilling life. Even if you're the only one who's heard the abuse, it still happened.

What Kind of Men Are Prone to Abuse Women?

Abusive men may initially appear to be the perfect partner. They may lavish a lot of attention on you during the courting phase and may let you know that, unlike his other partners, you are the one who can meet his needs. This can be very exciting and gratifying. After all, who is not looking to be "the one"? But abusers quickly become controlling, dominating, and abusive in the relationship because they hold a way of thinking about themselves and their partner that justifies their abuse and consistently excuses their actions. Lundy Bancroft, author of *Why Does He Do That? Inside the Minds of Angry and Controlling Men*, suggests that it is easy to believe an array of myths about abusive men and why they batter (they were battered as children, they have a hard time controlling their anger, they just explode and lose control). The bottom line is abusive men believe their actions are justified and they twist reality to explain and excuse their violence. Bancroft tells us that the real problem is the batterer's logic. They are in control of their anger and use their anger to control their partner. They often claim to be the "real" victim in a relationship because their partner failed to meet their unrealistic and unhealthy demands. Because batterers feel so entitled, they consistently fail to see their partner as someone who has her own needs or feelings or thoughts and will respond with rage if she asserts them. In his mind, she is simply wrong to have them. Men who batter not only do not have respect for their partners, but they often see them with contempt, as someone who is beneath them. And this justifies their control and their abuse.

Men who violate are so certain that they are justified in their behavior that they deny, minimize, and distort their behavior and its results. For them, they are not to blame, you are. Did you ever hear your partner try to minimize the way he hurt you? That's what we are talking about. This can sound like, "Well it wasn't that bad—I never hit her on her face," or "She just makes me so crazy I couldn't control myself," or "I only gave her what she had coming to her." No one who loves you, who can understand what violence feels like, and who wants to be in a mature loving relationship, would ever say these things. No one who loves you would ever demean you or fail to see you as the wonderful, strong, capable woman you are.

One of the hardest things to let go of when leaving an abusive relationship is the "if onlys"—if only I had worked harder, if only I had not burned the dinner, if only I had understood him better. These beliefs are hard to shake because the batterer has made believing them a condition of the relationship. He convinced you that the abuse was your fault, right? If only you had done or been something different then he wouldn't have been violent. And you spent a lot of time contorting yourself to fit his reality. But stop and realize that these "if onlys" point to a batterer's flawed thinking. You can't change that.

The battering was not your fault. You did not cause it or control it. You did not deserve it. Understanding why a man batters can help you understand what you were up against and can help you realize that the likelihood of your partner changing is low. Knowing this can help you move on.

Why Is It So Difficult to Leave an Abusive Relationship?

Understanding your personal history and how it might have contributed to you being in an abusive relationship are important parts of healing. This understanding is usually developed through individual therapy with an expert. It takes time and commitment and can be painful because it involves looking back at your experiences in your family of origin. But it is an important process because your history is probably part of the reasons you became involved with an abusive partner. Remember this: While your experiences in your family of origin may have helped set the stage for a relationship with a batterer, you *were not* and *are not* responsible for the early experiences that made you vulnerable to an abusive relationship. Understanding that it was not your fault, understanding that you are a wonderful human being who deserves love and who is capable of giving love in return is all a part of the healing journey.

Women who try to leave their abusers encounter a number of obstacles to leaving. The "barrier model," described by N. Grisby and B. R. Hartman in *Psychotherapy* magazine describes three "circles" of barriers that enclose a woman in an abusive relationship:

1. The outermost circle includes **environmental barriers** such as being unemployed, not having credit, any money, or even knowing how to handle money. It also includes not having a safe place to go in the community.
2. The next circle describes **family and social barriers** and can include lack of family support, and religious beliefs against divorce and separation.

3. The innermost circle describes **psychological barriers** a woman faces, such as fear for her own safety or the safety of her children, and still loving her partner.

For these reasons, we recognize how very difficult it was for you to leave your abusive relationship. Women we work with describe continued abuse and harassment even after they have left the abuser and they don't always find the support they need from the police and the criminal justice system. Finding employment, or going back to school and starting over can be a scary process. But the process of healing begins with recognizing the abuse, realizing you didn't and don't control the abuser, and understanding that you deserve a loving and supportive relationship.

Don't Go Backward

About one-third of women who leave an abuser will return, or enter into another abusive relationship. Be careful and pay attention to "red flags" when you begin to date. We recommend you wait quite awhile to begin dating. Dating puts your attention on someone else. Right now, you need and deserve all your attention on you. When the time comes for you to consider a relationship, here are some things to watch out for. Often, signs of the potential for an abusive relationship start to appear early in a relationship. It can happen on a first date, or when you are deeply in love. It can happen whether you are young or old, and in heterosexual or same-sex relationships. Watch out for a partner who commits these warning signs:

- Checks your cell phone or e-mail without permission
- Calls you numerous times during the day
- Exhibits extreme jealousy or insecurity
- Has an explosive temper
- Exerts financial control
- Isolates you from family or friends
- Has mood swings
- Physically hurts you or threatens you in any way
- Is possessive
- Stalks and spies on you
- Tells you what to do

Dating violence often starts with emotional abuse. You may think that behaviors like calling you names or insisting on seeing you all the time are a "normal" part of relationships. But they can lead to more serious kinds of abuse, like hitting, stalking, or preventing you from using birth control. You have worked so hard to get where you are today, don't fall into another abusive relationship. If you see any of these warning signs, or feel uncomfortable or threatened in any way, leave. Don't repeat the cycle of violence. Don't wait for him to change. That is his journey and he has to do that work before he can be in a healthy relationship. Remember, you deserve better. Stay true to your journey and keep your focus on you.

The Effects of an Abusive Relationship

An abusive relationship affects all aspects of your life: psychological, physical, and emotional. Your relationships with others have been altered as well. How you relate to friends, family, and your children has been impacted by violence. Let's look at some of the effects you may be dealing with in these areas and how to begin to address them.

The Psychological Effects of Abuse

Let's begin with some of the many ways that violation damages your psychological health.

Your Sense of Self

Feeling comfortable with others almost always begins with feeling comfortable with yourself. Have you ever heard women gossip or tear someone down behind her back? (Maybe even you've done this.) When you feel good about yourself, you don't do this. Though it seems counterintuitive, tearing someone else down comes from feeling bad about who *you* are. Here is why. We feel bad about ourselves because we are very aware of our own flaws and faults. The more we are aware of them, the worse we feel about ourselves. It is natural to want to turn away and not see them. So we shift our focus outward and see the flaws in others instead. Much of the time we also project our own flaws onto others. This makes us feel better; almost relieved. We can trick ourselves into thinking, "if so-and-so is bad, then it means that I am not so bad." But it is a mind trick. We all have flaws and faults. We all have work to do. The best way out of this hole is to take a look at the things you want to change in your life and about you. Be honest. Be fair. Be humble.

Feeling small, insecure, lost, afraid, angry, unworthy, and unlovable—as you probably do now, post-violation—can make finding a community of like-minded women hard because you simply bring old patterns of feeling, talking, thinking, and doing into a new environment and wonder why nothing is different.

Understanding how your sense of self has been affected can help you be aware of some of the things you might want to change about yourself, and then take steps toward facing that challenge. Once you begin to look inward and assess what you want to change you begin to attract people to you who are doing a similar work.

PTSD

One of the common psychological effects of an abusive relationship is post-traumatic stress disorder (PTSD). PTSD is a common psychological response that can occur during, just before, or after leaving an abusive relationship. Almost two-thirds of women who have been in abusive relationships experience PTSD. There are three main categories of PTSD symptoms:

1. The first category involves **reliving** or being preoccupied by the trauma. This can include nightmares, flashbacks, and the inability to stop thinking about the trauma.
2. The second category is a **fear response,** and includes emotional numbing, avoidant behaviors, and feeling detached. In this stage, it might be hard to "feel" anything.
3. The third category involves a **heightened response to everything**—high levels of arousal, difficulty concentrating, being tense, startling easily, and being cautious and hypervigilant (or super wary and suspicious) of your surroundings.

The effects of trauma and abuse are cumulative, that is to say, these effects of violence are increased and intensified by repeated exposure to it. The good news is that there are specialized therapeutic approaches that are effective in reducing the psychological impact of abuse, and the exercises and approach used in this workbook can also help.

"Learned Helplessness"

Another psychological effect of continued exposure to an abusive partner is a syndrome called "learned helplessness." This is a documented psychological response that occurs when a woman has been so beaten down that she no longer believes she has any control over her situation and cannot escape it. Another term for this is "learned powerlessness." This process is like brainwashing; it occurs over time and wears away at the woman's self-esteem and sense of self-worth.

When all of your energy is spent just trying to survive, you don't have a lot of time to reflect on what is happening around you. This book is about "unlearning" the expectations and demands of a batterer and relearning and reclaiming the power that was stolen from you in your past. It will be important for you to acknowledge and celebrate all the positive results that you set in motion through your actions—that's you reclaiming your power!

The Emotional Effects of Abuse

Depression and anxiety are psychological and emotional effects of abuse. Sometimes, women develop problems with alcohol or drugs as they try to cope with their emotions by numbing them. Others develop eating disorders as a reaction to low self-esteem or a sense of loss of control.

If you're in a situation like that, finding a way to fix the problem is essential before you can progress any farther in your healing journey. Here are some support options:

- Join a twelve-step recovery, or similar self-help program (such as Alcoholics Anonymous).
- Find a suitable spiritual group.
- Choose a therapist specializing in your specific situation. (If your relationships have been with alcoholics or addicts, that's an added dimension that a therapist could help with.)

Unhealthy coping affects you and your entire family. Finding appropriate help also allows you to meet and get help and insight from others who are trying to create similar changes and transformations in their lives.

The Physical Effects of Abuse

The visible physical results of abuse that you may be healing from are easier to see and feel, and they may seem more "legitimate" to those around you than some of the more subtle psychological effects.

Physical Manifestations of Depression

Hand in hand with the psychological effects of depression are some physical ones:

- Stomach/digestion problems
- Headaches/body aches
- Inability to sleep
- Changes in appetite
- Exhaustion

Physical Manifestations of Anxiety

Symptoms of anxiety keep your body in a constant state of heightened arousal, which can keep you from maintaining healthy sleep patterns. Your heart races, you sweat, you can even experience chest pain. The constant production of adrenaline by your body when you are anxious can cause aches and pains from tense muscles, headaches, and even nausea. The long-term effects of too much adrenaline can cause digestive problems, a weak immune system, and chronic, stress-related heart problems.

Alleviating Symptoms

Often it is a relief to hear that these physical symptoms are caused by depression or anxiety, because you can learn coping mechanisms to relieve them. Exercising and maintaining a healthy diet are two of the simplest and most effective ways to deal with depression and anxiety. This book will give you some tools for relieving the physical symptoms of depression and/or anxiety as you work through meditation and breathing exercises.

If, however, you are experiencing clinical depression or debilitating anxiety, you'll need professional help. The most effective treatments combine medication and therapy. The least helpful thing you can do is self-medicate by using drugs or alcohol. While it may seem easier to just numb up for a while, it actually complicates and lengthens the time you feel bad. Robert Frost, an American poet, is credited with saying, "The best way out is always through." While he may have been talking about country roads or a New England forest, he could have also been talking about you and your life and your feelings. Sometimes the only way out is all the way through. And this means feel the feelings you have. Work them through. Be done with them. You will feel a whole lot better than if you simply avoid them.

The Effects of Abuse on Your Family

Families who live with an abusive member are also affected by the abuse, whether or not they were subjected to violation. We have heard women say things like, "He was a good father. He never hit the kids." But if he was hitting you, yelling at you, kicking you, or in any way hurting you—then *he was hurting them too.* Children in the home can experience the same negative effects as the abused spouse: PTSD, depression, anxiety, and feelings of guilt or helplessness. And they can grow up to repeat the relationship patterns they have seen modeled in their home.

Therefore, your children will probably require professional help dealing with the impact of violence. A good resource for your children might be a school counselor or psychologist. Making the school aware of what is going on with your child is also important, so they can take it into account in terms of your child's behavior and academic program.

You may also be in the process of mending relationships outside your immediate family, or working through how those relationships played a part in the dynamics that you found yourself in. First, focus on your immediate family, and simply ask for support and love from family members that you feel safe asking. Avoid those who are not supportive until you get a little farther along in your recovery.

Stages of Recovering from an Abusive Relationship

Our Rites of Passage support groups for women recovering from a violating relationship have been offered in three different states and offered online. Through our work in these groups, we have identified four stages that are part of recovering, or reclaiming. We call it "reclaiming" because women are taking back what was stolen from them by their abusers.

Stage 1: Reclaim Your Place

The first is reclaiming place—both literally (a safe home to live in) and metaphorically (your sense of self). This is "a process, not an event," as the saying goes. You may have to live temporarily in one or more places before you get to that home. It may require a lot of work to be completely safe. Lack of money, loss of household items, restraining orders, and shared visitation with your children are a few of the problems you may be dealing with.

Reclaiming place for you might mean making the place where you are right now feel like your own, even if it's not. Do what you can to add items to your space that are completely you. Set up a place where you can practice meditation or relaxation techniques. If you need to establish a time when you can be alone in your space, see what you can do about child care. You may be able to swap babysitting time with someone else who has been wishing for some time alone too—she takes your kids one afternoon; you take hers another. These small changes can help you claim your temporary place while you are working toward finding one that is long term.

Stage 2: Reclaim Your Identity

The second stage is reclaiming your identity. This means being who you really are. This second stage intersects the first one, because you may not initially remember or know who that person is. You will have to reclaim yourself, and feeling safe is the first step toward this part of reclaiming.

Reclaiming your identity actually begins when you make the decision to leave an abusive relationship. You have chosen to stop letting someone else determine who you are. So the question now is: Who are you? One of the ways you can reconnect with your true self is to start a journal. You can start a page with "I Am . . ." and see where that takes you. You can also write a gratitude list, which is a list of all the things that you are grateful for, to find out what you truly value. This list might include items as simple as a sunrise, the smell of fresh-cut grass, or a day that passed without anyone hurting you or your children.

Other things you can do are to simply eat your favorite food or watch a movie that you know you love. By doing so, you're validating your choices as your own. Take yourself on a date to a park or a coffee shop or an art gallery, whatever you are interested in, and practice enjoying it again. Working with a support group and/or therapist is also an important part of reclaiming your identity.

Can you list three positive things that describe you?

I am . . .

_____

_____

I am . . .

_____

_____

I am . . .

_____

_____

Stage 3: Reclaim Your Life Path

The third phase involves reclaiming your life trajectory or path. When women enter into abusive relationships, they get stuck and don't grow and develop as they might otherwise. Giving up college or a career is an example of how life trajectory is interrupted and stalled during an abusive relationship. In order to survive in a violating relationship, all of your attention may have had to be on your abuser, on his wants, needs, and goals. Now, you will reclaim your right to rebuild your life.

Reclaiming your life trajectory might look a lot like reclaiming your identity. Journaling is an excellent tool for self-exploration. Ask yourself the question, "What do I want to be when I grow up?" and see what you find out. (It doesn't matter how old you are, this is always a great question!)

If you're stuck, start by looking backward. What did you want to be when you were younger? What dreams did you have to give up as a price for surviving life with someone who violated you? Can you reclaim those dreams now? Of course, your interests may have changed considerably since then, so don't be worried if they no longer fit your current ideas of what you would like to do.

A bigger issue might be gathering the time and resources you need to pursue that direction, whatever it is. Keep in mind that this is also a process, and it might take a lot of baby steps before you will find yourself moving freely along your reclaimed path. One possible effect of depression and PTSD is an inability to make decisions, and, in addition, therapists often advise against making big decisions in the middle of recovering, whether from a relationship or substance abuse, or both. If you need more time, simply continue to dream for awhile. Don't pressure yourself into making a decision just yet.

Stage 4: Reclaim Your Right to Your Future

The final stage is reclaiming the right to create your own future. This means developing the ability to recover a sense of hope and joy along with the expectations that the future holds good things for you. You are entitled to them.

There is a reason that reclaiming the right to create your own future is the final step. As you progressed through the first three parts of reclamation, you also started to work on the last, reclaiming your future. Through the activities and intro-spection that recovery requires, you experience little successes that build on each other. You can feel hope and joy as you experience these successes because you created them through your own hard work.

Humans can be conditioned to expect certain outcomes based on our experiences. If you have been experiencing a lot of disappointment or lack of control over your life, it will take time for you to begin to feel that you can expect good things. But it *can* happen. And it *can* happen for *you*.

Healing Unit 2

Reclaim Your Place

"Life isn't about finding yourself.
Life is about creating yourself."
—George Bernard Shaw

In this unit, you will:

- Assess how you feel now
- Address any lingering doubts or second-guessing you're experiencing
- Find a healthy support system
- Understand the differences among being a Victim, a Survivor, and a Thriver

How Do You Feel Now?

Given the immense challenges you faced leaving your relationship, your emotional state is likely in upheaval. You're probably experiencing myriad emotions, most of which are not very comfortable. You may feel a sense of fear as well as relief; you may have feelings of loss, depression, and helplessness.

Once some of those initial feelings begin to lessen, you might feel a more general sense that you lack direction and are confused about who you are, what you want in life, and how you might get it.

Does this sound like you? If so, you're like most women in the first stage of our healing process. You need to reclaim your place in the world.

ACTIVITY: *Your Feelings*

Take a minute now to list all the feelings you're currently experiencing.

_____

_____

_____

_____

_____

_____

_____

_____

_____

_____

You might have to spend some energy grieving your losses—the loss of a relationship, the loss of a place to live, the loss of tenderness mixed into a confusing and sometimes scary relationship. Think about it: Living in a violating relationship tied up all your energy simply surviving. Now that energy is available. You may wish to use that energy to grieve your losses and take care of your other feelings.

ACTIVITY: *What Do You Miss?*

What do you miss about your relationship and your former life? Were there romantic dates? Did he make you laugh at times? The things you miss might be some of the elements you may want to hold on to and create for yourself in your new life. Only this time, without the violation. Go ahead and make that list.

_____

_____

_____

_____

_____

_____

_____

_____

_____

_____

_____

_____

_____

ACTIVITY: *What Do You Need?*

You've probably become very good at taking care of other people's feelings and needs, especially the person who violated you. You may have even seen this as your job or your reason for living. But you have a new job now and it is one of the most important you will ever have: Take care of yourself and your kids, if you have them. So think for a minute about what you need in order to do that. In your journal answer the following questions:

What are some things that would help *me* feel better right now?

_____

_____

_____

_____

What are some things that might help *my kids* feel better right now?

_____

_____

_____

_____

What decisions must I make right away to help me feel better?

_____

_____

_____

_____

Challenging Second-Guessing Head-On

Whether you have just left an abusive relationship or you have been out of it for a while, you may still be questioning whether you made the right decision, or asking yourself, *was it really* that *bad?* You may still be wondering, *was it really abuse? Was it my fault that the abuse happened?* For many of us, leaving an abusive situation can make things more difficult for a while, until we become more comfortable in our new lives. Fear of the unknown can make you question your decision.

In addition, you may have a case of the "what ifs." They sound like this:

- "What if I didn't . . ."
- "What if I hadn't . . ."
- "He wouldn't have hit me if I didn't . . ."
- "If the kids had just been quieter, he wouldn't have . . ."

The fact is, you deserve better than what you had. And loving relationships are not painful.

Don't Make Excuses for Him

Loving relationships also shouldn't need to be qualified. For example, you shouldn't have to say things like, "He was a great guy, unless he was drinking." Or "He was a good dad to his own kids," or "He was only really mean when he had a bad day at work." These are qualifiers. The truth is, you can find a partner who loves you, loves your kids, and respects you all—without qualification. People have bad days at work all the time and don't come home and hit the people they love. People drink all the time and don't turn into frightening, unreasonable abusers.

If the relationship could have been different, it would have been. If he could have been different, he would have been. If he could have changed, he would have (even if he always promised he would). The truth is, he just couldn't be anyone other than who he was. And that meant being someone who was abusive.

ACTIVITY: *Leftover "What Ifs?"*

"What ifs" can paralyze you or put you in a state of inaction. You can't move forward because "what if" thinking keeps one foot in the past. Are there any "what ifs" you think about that we haven't mentioned? Write them down now. It is important to get these thoughts out of your head and on paper where you can face them.

_____

_____

_____

_____

_____

_____

Once you get them on paper, answer them just the way we have in this part of the book. For example, you might write, "What if I had cooked more food he liked?" Answer that "what if" with some realistic, clear thinking. It will sound like this: "No matter what I cooked, I never deserved to be beaten or yelled at. Loving men simply don't behave like that."

_____

_____

_____

_____

_____

_____

_____

_____

_____

_____

_____

Can He Change?

Research tells us that men who batter hold entrenched ways of thinking about relationships and women. If they do change, it is because *they initiated it* and worked very hard to accept responsibility for their own behavior. If your partner hasn't done that kind of work yet, chances are he can't change at this point. He isn't ready to change and his promises, no matter how much he means them at the time, mean nothing. He simply can't deliver. If he meant to deliver, he would have gotten himself into counseling. Lundy Bancroft, in a Pandora's Project blog (*www.pandys.org/lundybancroft-transcript.html*), gives us this list of signs that an abuser is not changing:

1. He tells you that you should be appreciating how much he has changed.
2. He says "I can't be perfect" as an excuse to keep doing abusive things.
3. He thinks it's okay to keep being abusive, as long as the incidents are farther apart than they used to be (e.g., he

says, "You are so upset with me, and I haven't done anything like that in a long time—I've been really good").

4. He tells you that now it's time for you to focus on the changes that you need to make.
5. He is disconnecting from you emotionally—in other words, the reason he is being less abusive is that he is simply not being anything very much—he's withdrawn.
6. He is continuing to make excuses.
7. He says "We're getting along better," which means that as soon as you start to stand up to him or challenge him forcefully again, he'll be going right back to his old ways.
8. He still gets impatient when you try to talk to him in a serious way about the things that are really important to you in life, including your desires for the relationship.

If they sound familiar, then you know that he is not able or ready to change. If he can't change, that means the only way to break the cycle of violation is for you to initiate the change. By leaving and getting yourself to safety, you did the only thing you could do to protect yourself and your children.

Facing the Emptiness

Leaving a relationship—even an unhealthy one—leaves a big, deep, empty feeling inside of you. Once some of the initial relief wears off, you begin to feel empty, sad, alone, and really frightened and unsure if you can survive alone. This is a time when women begin to look for ways to fill up this void.

Newsflash: That void or emptiness is actually a *good* thing. You need to grieve the loss of someone who loved you and someone you loved. You need to grieve the loss of a way of living. It is okay to feel sad, lonely, and lost. But the only way to come out of it is to go through it.

Trying to fill up that emptiness with another relationship only means that you covered over those feelings you have. They are still there and need taking care of. And you haven't had time to figure out who you are and what you can bring to a new and loving relationship. Before you go into a new relationship, you need to reclaim yourself.

Think about a glass half full of water. By looking for a new relationship shortly after a breakup, a lot of women look for someone who can fill up their glass. Their "cup" feels empty and they hope a new relationship or a man can help them feel complete or whole. But the problem is, they often attract someone who also feels empty and lost and is looking to be filled up and made complete; someone who also has work to do.

To avoid that situation, stop and do your work now. Take care of those empty, sad, and lonely feelings and then begin to look for a relationship. Then you can attract another human being who is also complete or full. A relationship you find after doing this work by grieving your losses and reclaiming yourself means that you come to a relationship complete and whole and able to share all of you.

ACTIVITY: *Write a Gratitude List*

One way to help yourself remember to count the positives in your life is to keep a list of the positives in your journal. What should you put on this list? Everything! "I took a shower today and fixed my hair." "I went for a walk in the park." "I decided to lose a pound." Anything that is a positive event that you have initiated in your life goes on this list. There will be bigger and better things to add to the list as time goes on and you begin to expect and feel that you deserve them. But we start walking with baby steps. We start making changes one tiny change at a time.

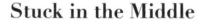

Stuck in the Middle

When we go through important life transitions, we inevitably reach a point where we must leave behind the old and embrace the new. In a way, this is like straddling two worlds. You know the life you are leaving, but the life ahead of you may not look as crystal clear. You may even doubt that something new and different and better is out there for you, or doubt that you are doing the right thing. Uncertainty can be tough at this stage.

Anthropologists, people who study the way human beings live and make meaning, study these transitions. They learned that in many non-Western societies, as children grow up, they have to leave the life of a child behind and learn the ways of being an adult. In some communities, this means going to a special school or receiving special instructions and is often marked by a physical separation from family and other younger children. After that instruction, the participants perform a ritual or have a ceremony in which their new status is recognized by the community. Through this ritual, all members in their society understand that they are no longer relating to children or adolescents but are now welcoming new adult members to the group. The participants declare to the world that they are no longer children and everyone in their community recognizes this shift and begins to treat them like adults.

Anthropologists call this time when children are learning how to become an adult liminality. Participants are no longer children since they are learning a new role, but they aren't yet adults either. They can see the new role that lies ahead of them and they are learning it, but they are not quite there. In a way, they're in a "neither here nor there" stage—stuck in the middle, so to speak.

Parallels to Your Journey

If you think about it, the journey you are on has some interesting parallels to what anthropologists found in many non-Western societies. Once you left your abuser, you separated yourself from the life you had known. Once you made that change, you entered a period of liminality, where you had to learn a whole new way of being. You had to learn how to live without violation and live instead in its wake. During this period, you had to figure out what it means to be a Survivor and to grasp what it could mean to be a Thriver.

This in-between period is especially difficult because you have the distinct feeling you are not yet where you want to be, despite all the brave changes you have made thus far. You may feel "unfinished" or "in process." You may still struggle with a lot of issues brought about by violation, like trust and worthiness. And you may feel lonely and remember the good times that you had with your abuser. At this point, some women slip back into old patterns and either enter another relationship where they are mistreated or go back to their abuser. Sometimes the devil we know is less frightening than the devil we do not. It is scary to learn new skills and new ways of living especially since no one has handed you a clearly marked map and since you may question whether or not you should be on this path in the first place.

The Only Way Out Is Through

While you are going through the liminal phase, it is easy to project a "tough girl" image and to keep a protective wall around you to prevent more hurt. This protection helped you survive in the past, after all. But as you move forward, you may find that you are outgrowing this wall and can replace it with healthy boundaries.

When you feel "stuck in the middle," you may also try to find comfort in alcohol or drugs. You're the boss, so you will have to decide what you do and how much. But here is a word of caution from those of us who have been where you are. Healing comes with its unique pain and it is tempting to numb up or zone out for a while. But the numbness you get from drinking or drugging is short term and can impede your journey. A long-term solution is to work through the pain—get to the other side and be done with it rather than simply numbing it out and then having to return to it when the substance wears off.

Danielle likens it to an experience she had when she moved into a new house. Her house was a mess, full of unpacked boxes and out-of-place furniture. Instead of unpacking, she decided to take a trip to give herself a break from the stress of moving. When she returned a week later, she found the house still in chaos, full of boxes that needed to be unpacked and furniture that needed to be placed. A week had passed but, unfortunately, she returned to the same place she had left. While she got a temporary break from chaos and the drudgery of setting up house, had she stayed and worked at it for that week she would have gotten her house in order. It would have been done.

The same is true for substance use. If you can stay with the journey, you can work through the pain and get to a place where you feel really great. If you keep checking out—even for a while—you will be slowed down and you will prolong your healing. It is a struggle to emerge from the in-between state, but you have already taken the first steps.

You are on a path that other women have been on and one that will turn out very well. Understanding that something wonderful can and *does* lie ahead for you, and knowing that you are on the verge of getting there can make this stage a little easier to navigate. Know this: You deserve love without violation and you will find love because you are lovable. You deserve happiness and you will find happiness because you are a good person, no matter what mistakes you made in your life.

Nothing you have ever done can change the fact that you are a wonderful person.

ACTIVITY: *Leaving the Middle*

Even though what you left wasn't good for you, or was downright painful, it probably had some good elements to it. Now is the time to decide what healthy aspects you want to bring with you from your old life into your new life. If your partner loved you tenderly at times, but also violated you, you might want to identify a loving relationship that has no violation.

In this activity, look at the good things you left behind when you left a violating relationship. Identify the feelings you had about it. Then think about whether you want this in your new life and what it might look like. Take a look at the example below, then add your own.

What I left behind	How I feel about that	What I wish for my new life
Example: a place to live and the assurance that rent would be paid	*Example:* secure	*Example:* my own place to live and enough money to pay the rent every month

What I left behind	How I feel about that	What I wish for my new life

Find Your Community

Since you have taken the first step in your healing process and have left your abusive relationship, you've created a safe place for the rest of your journey to unfold. That space now needs to be filled with healing, reassuring, and positive influences. These factors can help you when you feel particularly vulnerable to doubt, second-guessing, or sadness.

You have probably heard a person described in three parts: mind, body, spirit. We suggest that there is a fourth, which is environment. And it is as important as the other three.

Take the steps now to find a supportive environment—a community, a place where you feel safe, a place where people can understand what you have been through and who you are, and who will give you the support that will allow you to work on mind, body, and spirit. You might find this in your current living arrangement. Or it might be in a church or with volunteers for a project. Our point is—look for this.

What Is a Community?

Sometimes finding that community is a long process. The first place you find might not be the best place for you, and it might be stressful to be there. It might take time for you to:

- Find the right support group
- Decide on the right living arrangements
- Choose the right therapist who you can work with
- Identify which friends truly value you and your family's safety and well-being

No matter how long it takes, don't give up. These are all aspects of your environment that, when they are positive, will support growth and change in your mind, body, and spirit. Once you find that place where people can know, love, and understand you for who you are, the "barriers" described earlier can be transformed into circles of support.

Obstacles to Finding a Community

Despite your best efforts to find healthy influences, years of unhealthy interactions with others because of abusive relationships can create barriers. You might have been isolated and unable to create meaningful friendships with other women. You might have used and abused substances to help you cope. You have become an expert at keeping people away from you.

One of the ways that women cope with abuse is to build walls. These walls keep everybody out and this includes potential women friends. Other women can be seen as threatening for many reasons:

- Maybe you were afraid she would notice the abuse and you would have to talk to her about it.
- Maybe your abuser threatened leaving you for someone else as part of his control over you.
- Maybe another relationship of any kind was beyond your ability because you were so worn out from dealing with your abusive one.

On the other hand, sometimes you may have maintained relationships that you *thought* benefited you or helped you deal with your situation, especially if you were using substances to cope. In reality, however, these relationships were not healthy ones either. For example, you may have had "bar friends" or a female friend who supplied you with drugs.

Starting a new life often begins with time spent in a communal living situation. You may be in a women's shelter or transitional housing while you get back on your feet. You are living with other women who have been through many of the same experiences that you have, and they have built the same walls and learned the same unhealthy coping skills. All of those personalities can create a competitive, hostile, defensive environment. How are you supposed to turn this into your new community?

Break Down Your Walls

The first step toward letting in positive influences, particularly other women, is to start bringing down those walls. Open yourself up to a conversation, ask if you can help someone with something, or offer a cup of coffee or a chair. We, as women, are often good at building community and nurturing others. Build on those strengths. Bake cookies for everyone; establish a movie night or game night; have a "girls' night" complete with manicures and junk food. These new activities will help you get to know your community, break down those walls, and enjoy a supportive friendship simply for the companionship. When you get together with other women, make a conscious effort to find one strength or positive quality in each woman. It's not always easy to recognize the positive, especially coming out of such a negative relationship. Just keep working at it.

These actions also create new pathways in your thinking. Instead of shutting down and closing everyone out, you're showing your brain a new way to approach life. These activities and the company of others in your community may feel strange at first. This is one of those times when you may have to "act your way" into breaking down your walls. For example, start a conversation even if you're shy or not sure you'll say the right thing. Invite some women over to watch TV even if you aren't sure you will have a good time. It is important to try some new things.

Tearing down the walls and working on building your community is hard work, but it is very rewarding and ultimately can support your new life. Remember the quote from Martin Luther King Jr., in the last unit. The way we climb a whole flight of stairs is one step at a time. And we promise the whole staircase is there.

How Healing Happens: Moving from Victim to Survivor to Thriver

Similar to a physical wound that heals gradually, your emotional wounds also follow a gradual path. Healing typically occurs in predictable stages, which you are just beginning now, as you reclaim your place. In Unit 1, we introduced some of the feelings and symptoms you may have encountered or are encountering now. Now, we're placing those feelings into more concrete stages of healing. Learning about these stages can help you assess and understand how you're feeling and determine the next logical step for you to take to reclaim your place in your own life.

Stage 1: Victim

When you first left your abuser, you may have felt raw, afraid, and depressed. These emotions are typical in the Victim stage. This is the stage where you need to find safety, perhaps at a women's shelter, and figure out how you will put one foot in front of the other to simply get through each day. If you were physically hurt, this is the stage in which your body heals. Living in a violating relationship is stressful and stress can wreak havoc with your body. You probably had to put everyone's needs before your own, including your physical needs. Now, you must put your own needs first. To do that, it is essential that you find out and communicate to others what you need right now.

What to Do in This Stage
If you're in this stage, here are some things you can do:

- Get checked out medically. Most communities have free or low-cost health care options. If you were not able to bring needed medications when you left, this would be a good time to get a new prescription rather than trying to recover ones still in your home.
- Talk with a women's shelter advocate or a therapist. They can walk you through the numerous immediate decisions that lie ahead of you.
- Determine what specific needs you have to address immediately. Do you need a restraining order? Child care? A place to live? A job? Make a list and prioritize it.

How to Ask for Help
It can be difficult to actually tell someone what you need, but it is worth your energy. Many women in your situation are used to shutting others out, not asking for help. Here are some things you might try.

- Start small, but be specific.
- Try starting with a trusted family member or friend. Your request might sound like this: "Now that I've left Bob, I have to take some steps to get my life back on track. You've been such a good friend to me, I wonder if I could ask you for some help. I really need a place to stay until I can find my own apartment."
- Consider asking for help from a social service agency. Start with the YWCA in your community. Be specific about

what you need: "I am looking for shelter. I have left an abusive relationship and need help."

After you have been checked out medically and determined what your immediate needs are, you will still need to give yourself time to heal. Living with the stress and anxiety and fear that a long-term violating relationship can bring about can leave you feeling exhausted and numb, or unable to sleep and overwhelmed. No matter how bleak it seems, you will get through this stage by taking one day at a time and getting help.

Stage 2: Survivor

Over time and with support, you may have noticed that you are doing better than you had initially. This is the Survivor stage. You may have found a place to live, gotten a restraining order, or started divorce proceedings. You might have also found a way to support yourself and your family and begun to establish a predictable order to your days.

Talk It Out

During this stage, on an emotional level, you may struggle to make sense of your experiences and find that it helps to tell your story to people who understand you. Women in the Survivor stage often benefit from talking with a therapist, a good friend who's been through this before, or a support group of women who have been through similar experiences. Doing so may help you to look at your relationship patterns and make sense of your past experiences with violation, some of which may have been repeated numerous times.

Most women's shelters have support groups that are free and open to any woman who needs them. If you haven't already received shelter services, call your local YWCA.

Moving Forward

While you may feel relieved that you are no longer being violated, you may also still feel depressed, empty, and a little lost. You know where you have been, but you have no idea where you are going. Questions, like *How am I going to support myself?*, *Where am I going to live?*, and *How will I pay the rent?* take a lot of your energy. And you may be missing the comfort and love you got from your partner when things were going well.

In this stage, many of your physical wounds have healed, and a lot of women find they are able to put one foot in front of the other and get through each day with a little more confidence. That newfound sense might lead you to feel like you no longer need a support group—yet you may have moments when you still feel lonely, a little empty, and scared inside. It's not uncommon to straddle stages as you heal, or to take one step forward and two steps backward. Acknowledge these feelings when they arise—they're a normal part of the healing process. The key is to keep moving forward, even if it's with baby steps.

We have also found that at a certain point in your healing, it is no longer helpful to tell your story of victimization. Instead it is time to develop a new story about who you are and where you are going. Developing a new story about who you are and where you are heading and actively working toward making that story come true is one of the most important ways to move from the Survivor to the Thriver stage.

Stage 3: Thriver

In the Thriver stage, you are beginning to feel healed, whole, complete, and satisfied with yourself and your accomplishments. You no longer define yourself in terms of your violation (for example, "I am a survivor of violence" or "I am a victim of violence"). Instead, you see yourself as a thriving, successful, happy, and fulfilled woman in spite of (or maybe because of) your experiences with violation. Getting you to the Thriver stage is the goal of this book.

In our work with the Rites of Passage groups, we found that there are certain key hallmarks of the Thriver stage:

1. **Establishing your own home.** Once you've left a violating relationship, it can take awhile to set up a home that is a personal expression of your unique style. The process takes hard work, money, and time. Plus, it might have been a very long time since you were able to even think about what you like and what you prefer. Once you're a Thriver, you are able to make independent choices and follow through on them. Your home is one significant reflection of that triumph.

2. **Becoming more independent and confident.** With a newfound sense of freedom, you are able to take risks, and make mistakes and learn from them. By taking action and responsibility for your own life, you grow. Once you've left a violating relationship, you can begin to figure out who you are and who you want to be. This might mean going back to school or finding a job or handling your own money. It also means making decisions about your life that are good for you—like what kind of movies you want to see or how you spend your free time.

3. **Taking care of yourself physically, emotionally, and spiritually.** Doing this will allow you to reclaim your life, and pursue your goals and dreams. This might mean finding a supportive religious community for Bible study or fellowship, reserving one night a week just for yourself and a bubble bath, or joining other women who are trying to lose weight.

Of course, you don't just wake up one morning and think, "Hmmm. I am a Thriver today." This is a process, and it can be very gradual with some ebb and flow to it.

Victim, Survivor, Thriver at a Glance

Barbara Harris Whitfield, a therapist and author of several books on spirituality and healing, has conceptualized the three stages of healing and offered an example of what we might experience. We have adapted her work into the chart that follows for a quick way to assess where you stand. See if you recognize yourself in any of these stages. You can read the chart either across in rows or read each of the columns. You might also observe that you have moved back and forth between the stages.

Three Stages of Healing

VICTIM	SURVIVOR	THRIVER
Believes she doesn't deserve nice things or doesn't deserve to try for the "good life"	Struggles for reasons and chance to heal	Is grateful for everything in life
Has low self-esteem, feels shame and feels unworthy	Sees self as wounded and healing	Sees self as an overflowing miracle
Is hypervigilant (this means feeling on guard all of the time, feeling like there is always a threat around the next corner)	Seeks help and believes she deserves to seek help and names what happened to her; uses tools to learn to relax	Feels gratitude for her new life
Feels alone, selfish, damaged, confused, numb, and hopeless	Begins to feel hopeful	Feels a sense of oneness with others and with the universe; also feels proud of herself and her ability to care for herself
Is overwhelmed by past	Is learning to grieve the past and those painful experiences from the past	Was wounded and is now healing
Uses outer world to hide from self	Comes out of hiding to hear others and have compassion for them and eventually self	Lives in the present and has faith in herself and life. Understands that emotional pain will pass and brings new insights
Hides her story from others and believes everyone else is better, stronger, less damaged	Is not afraid to tell her story to safe people	Is beyond telling her story, but always aware she has created her own healing

Three Stages of Healing

VICTIM	SURVIVOR	THRIVER
Is often wounded by being around others who are unsafe	Is learning how to protect self by checking her perceptions of safety or danger with others	Protects self from unsafe others and lives with an open heart
Places own needs last	Learns what healthy needs are and how to meet them	Places self first realizing that is the only way to function and eventually help others
Creates one drama after another	Sees patterns in her life that she wants to change	Creates peace
Believes suffering is the human condition	Feels some relief; knows the need to continue in recovery	Finds joy in peace
Is serious all the time and has trouble feeling joy	Begins to laugh	Sees the humor in life
Uses inappropriate humor, including teasing	Feels associated painful feelings instead	Uses healthy humor
Is uncomfortable, numb, or angry around toxic people	Has increased awareness of pain and the relationship dynamics that caused the pain	Creates healthy boundaries around toxic people, including relatives
Lives in the past	Starts to be aware of patterns in her life	Lives in the now
Is angry at religion	Understands the difference between religion and personal spirituality	Enjoys personal relationship with the God of her understanding

Three Stages of Healing		
VICTIM	**SURVIVOR**	**THRIVER**
Suspicious of therapists and places her own feelings onto others	Sees a therapist as a guide and explores the way she might be projecting her feelings onto others	Owns her own reality
Needs people and chemicals to believe she is all right	Stays with emotional pain and begins to glimpse self-acceptance and fun without substances and without others	Feels authentic, connected, and whole
Feels depressed	Begins to feel a wider range of feelings other than just depression	Feels a range of positive and negative feelings and feels alive

Original chart © 2003 by Barbara Whitfield. Adaptations made with permission.

Did you recognize the stages you have been through? Did you recognize some of the ways of seeing the world? Don't be surprised if you saw yourself in all three columns. Our journey toward thriving is not necessarily an all-or-nothing proposition nor is it ever a straight line. The important thing to know is that as you heal, you can and will steadily move toward life as a Thriver. In addition, you will stay in the Thriver space longer and more consistently. The activities in this unit help strengthen the skills necessary to see yourself as a Thriver.

ACTIVITY: *Victim, Survivor, Thriver Energy*

Revisit the Victim, Survivor, Thriver chart you just read. Using the chart below, write three things in each column about what you did or felt as a Victim, how you experienced the same thing as a Survivor, and what you are doing or will do as a Thriver.

For example:

As a Victim, I . . .	As a Survivor, I . . .	As a Thriver, I Will . . .
Was filled with shame about being violated.	Told my story to other women who had similar experiences and found I was not alone.	Help other women get connected to support groups that can help them in their journey. I will also let other women know they are not alone.

When you are done, take what you have written in the Thriver column and create one or more affirmations. Based on the example shown, an affirmation may be:

I help other women on their journey to know what to expect.
I am hopeful and I offer others hope.
I am helpful.
I am connected to others.
I am empathetic.

Now write your Thriver affirmations:

_____
_____
_____
_____
_____
_____
_____
_____
_____
_____
_____
_____
_____
_____

Your Healing Journey Will Become Less Painful

When we think about healing and healing experiences, we often associate the process with pain. Think about it: When you go to the dentist to get a tooth repaired, it is painful; surgery to repair something in your body can be painful. Even mental health therapy to help you feel better emotionally can be painful.

More specifically to the process of overcoming a violation, the process can be painful as well. The type of healing you had to do in the Victim stage was probably pretty unpleasant. You had to look backward at yourself, your family, and your experiences and work through some tough feelings. The work you had to do to become a Survivor was difficult too, and you probably experienced painful moments of recognition and insight.

The type of healing that comes in the Thriver stage is different, however. While it can be a lot of work with some bumps in the road, generally, this stage of healing actually turns on joy, hope, and creativity. Once you reach this stage, you can begin to have fun, enjoy what you are doing, and be creative. You'll have the confidence to try new things. You might want to start drawing, painting, or writing. In fact, these creative activities are an important part of the work at the Thriver stage. Through expansive thinking, you can reconnect with:

- Your playful self
- The unlimited possibility of your imagination

- Your power to create the rules for the world you want to live in

Reawakening these parts of yourself is how you heal.

ACTIVITY: *Build a Picture of Thriving*

In this activity, you will create a collage from magazine clippings or with your own drawings to produce an image of what Thriving looks like to you. At first you might feel like you're making a kid's art project, but that couldn't be farther from the truth! Seeing images of Thriving will help you project yourself into your future. These images help forge neural pathways upon which to premise additional goals and ultimately behavioral change. It is a first step in using your imagination to visualize that third, Thriver stage for yourself. When you create your future in pictures, you are better able to reproduce that image or imagined experience in real life.

What you might use: magazines (you can get these from friends or oftentimes the public library has free outdated magazines), scissors, gluestick, glitter, markers, paper, photographs. At the top of your collage write:

"I Thrive!"

Now create a collage that illustrates this for yourself.

A Time to Reflect

Reflection on the steps we take toward Thriving is important. By frequently taking stock of the changes you are making, you can be mindful of the changes that intentionally come from you and are becoming a part of you. You call the shots for this leg of your life journey. Though you want to focus on moving forward, stopping to look at the progress you've made is a great way to celebrate your successes and identify your next steps.

Reflecting on the changes you have made so far is an important step in recognizing those thoughts and beliefs that are new to you. It also helps as a benchmark on your journey.

ACTIVITY: *Reflecting*

Think back on the activities you completed in this unit to discover which has been the most helpful for you. Can you put into words why it was helpful? Recognizing what helped you make important changes means that you can focus on that piece to help you make future changes. You might also reflect on the transformation you have experienced in your life right now and celebrate it.

_____

_____

_____

_____

_____

_____

_____

What has changed for you?

_____

_____

_____

_____

What new picture or image of yourself is emerging?

_____

_____

_____

_____

How have your thoughts changed?

_____

_____

_____

_____

What has changed in your living, work, or family environment? For example, did you get a job? Do you have a new place to live?

_____

_____

_____

_____

What activities do you want to repeat and why?

_____

_____

_____

_____

Which activity taught you the most about yourself?

_____

_____

_____

_____

How might you celebrate or mark the changes you've made so far?

_____

_____

_____

_____

Reclaim Your Identity

"Go confidently in the direction of your dreams. Live the life you have imagined!"
HENRY DAVID THOREAU

In this unit, you will:

- Get acquainted with the healing process
- Understand how to transition between healing stages
- Reclaim your personal power and energy
- Create a new story about your life
- Use your imagination to change your thinking

Reharnessing Your Power

In an abusive relationship, the loss of power that you experienced is the main challenge you'll face as you reclaim your identity. It's natural at this point to focus on what you probably *don't* currently have: a romantic relationship, financial stability, a long-term housing plan, maybe even a career. Instead, think for a minute about what you *do* have: a safe life, the chance to make your life the way *you* want it, a promising outlook for you and your children.

When you acknowledge and celebrate the power and bravery it took to break free, you're planting the seeds of your new identity. In this section we will help you feel that power as your own, determine its source, and begin to expand it. This is a part of reclaiming your identity. We will also help you reawaken dreams that may have been sidetracked by simply surviving in a violating relationship.

Where Did Your Power Go?

For just a moment let's think about some of the many ways that violation can impact a woman's ability to maintain power over her own life.

- Violation robbed you of your power and your selfhood. You may have learned that there was nothing you could do to stop the violation you experienced, so you developed ways to live with it, taking the good (love, nurturing, and the way he needed you) with the bad (the physical or emotional beatings).
- Violation also robs you of your natural compass, and therefore robs you of your sense of direction and your balance.

The imposed reality of your violator turns reality upside down, making what is wrong, right and what is right, wrong. We all need and want to be loved completely and well. But when you are in an abusive relationship, no matter what you do you cannot get the kind of love you are seeking because men who violate women are not capable of giving love in the way most of us need it.

- Although you could not stop your partner from violating you, you likely believed you could, making the situation "your fault." By believing this fallacy, you lost sight of your self, your own needs, desires, skills, and self-sufficiency. And you lost sight of the truth—your truth.

- When you spend your time trying to please or placate another person, trying to prove to someone that you are not the damaged person he or she believes you to be, you erode your power. Through this gradual process your gifts and selfhood are buried alive.

- You may also have accepted the upside-down worldview and a slew of "rules" the violator established as a condition of love. For example, you may have learned to accept an image of yourself as broken, unworthy, or unlovable. You may have learned to feel shame that you were being violated rather than letting the violator feel shame for his or her behavior. You may have also learned to maintain secrets that were not yours to keep in order to protect the violator. Furthermore, you may have learned that in order to be loved, you had to suppress your own sense of self and give up your power.

- Focusing on the actions of your violator causes you to lose sight of yourself and accept the idea that you are not important. In a violating relationship, you have to focus on the violator because he/she demands it as a condition of love and because it is a way for you to survive. However, this caused you to feel smaller and more insignificant, and in contrast, your abuser gained more power. The more you focus on something, the more energy you bring to it, and the bigger it becomes in your life. In order to survive, you gave power to the violator. Like a teeter-totter that is out of balance, the more powerless you felt, the more powerless you acted, and the more powerful the violator felt. Feeling and acting powerless created a reality in which you *were* powerless.

Physical Manifestations of Powerlessness

There is also a physical component to powerlessness, because your mind and body are inseparably connected. Your feelings are the road between the two—they are the way in which your mind and body understand and communicate with each other. Think of the relationship as a triangle: One side is your feelings, one is your thoughts, and the third side is your body. When you are stressed or otherwise in crisis, your mind reacts by recognizing the danger and sending a signal to your body. You feel scared or threatened and then tighten up in order to defend yourself. This is a natural instinct; you are protecting yourself by preparing to either fight or run away.

Sometimes, though, you cannot fight and you cannot run away, so your body learns to live in a constant state of stress, waiting for the next crisis or explosion to occur. Your ability to adapt and survive in this kind of a stressful environment is truly amazing, but it comes at a high cost—loss of self, negative thinking, and depression. Once the stress has been removed, it can be difficult to adapt to life without constant stress or other threats to your well-being. But now that you have left a battering relationship, it is time to reclaim what was taken from you. This reclamation is healing.

Free Yourself

One way to get your power back is to leave your violator, but this is not the only thing you need to do. To reclaim your power, you need to develop a different way of thinking about yourself, your abilities, your worth, and your future.

You Can Break Free from Your Chain

This story, explained in Gavin de Becker's book *The Gift of Fear*, helps illustrate what we mean. Young elephants are trained to stay in one place by chaining one of their legs to a sturdy tree. The young elephant struggles for days and weeks to break free from this chain until it realizes the chain cannot be broken and it gives up trying. Once an elephant reaches adulthood, however, it could easily break free, but the elephant's experiences with the limits of the chain make it believe that it cannot be free and thus it accepts captivity as its truth and reality. This story illustrates that we live what we learn. It also suggests that some of the life lessons you have learned—especially those about your own powerlessness—are not true and must be unlearned if you are to change your reality and reclaim your identity.

Redirecting Your Defensive Energy

Imagining yourself as a powerful person again can be disorienting at first. Your mind and body remain prepared for the next assault because they have been trained to do so. It is easy to react rather than act or to *over*react, since you are ready for the fight. This is defensive energy and it pushes people away from you. When you are defensive, you radiate your readiness for a fight. Since no one wants to fight, people will gravitate away from you. This defensive energy helped you survive in an abusive relationship, but it will keep you lonely and isolated when you are trying to reclaim your identity. As you shift from Surviving to Thriving, you will see that there is no fight and you can instead invest that defensive energy in creative endeavors.

The Power of You

The process of reharnessing your personal power also encourages you to shift your attention back to yourself. This shift transforms the world from a hostile and unfriendly place to a world full of unlimited possibilities. As you learn to create a life based on Thriving, here are some new truths to help with the shift in your thoughts and your behavior.

- **You cannot control other people. Not really. Not ever. You cannot, nor could you ever, control the person who violated you. But you control yourself and the choices you make now.** Put the focus back on you to begin your journey to reclaim your power, your soul, and your path. You did not deserve to be violated. Not ever. Not by anyone. That is not your fate; that is not your destiny. Your destiny is to be loved and loved well, and you can and will reconnect with that life path.

- **You could not and cannot control how your violator loved you. But you control how you will be loved from this day forward.** You can find the kind of love you need and deserve. Love does not come with violation.

- **You cannot, nor could you ever, control who your violator thought you were. But you control how you respond to people who violate.** And you can control who you are and who you become. People who violate tend to see others through a lens of their own insecurity, need, fears, and sense of unworthiness. You can't control how someone else thinks of you. But you can keep who you are—a wonderful, healing woman who deserves love and respect—in the front of your thoughts at all times.

- **You cannot control what other people want and need in this world or what they get. But you control what you need and want and you most certainly can control what you are going to get out of life.** You must simply reclaim your power and identity. Rather than remaining an expert on your abuser and his or her needs and wants, put your focus back on you, on what you need, and want, and feel. In other words, you kept your focus on the abuser because you had to. But you don't have to anymore. Become an expert on yourself again. In this unit we will start small and give you lots of practice.

You Deserve Happiness!

This book is founded on the principle that you were not brought into this world to suffer. You were brought into this world to be happy and fulfilled. In fact, it is your birthright to be happy. Think about that for a minute. You were born to be happy. You are a profoundly wonderful, gifted, and perfect human being. Accepting this reality is a key part of reclaiming your identity and sense of personal power.

When you were created, you were given everything you needed for a wonderful life. Even if it doesn't feel like it at the moment, you have it now. It is all inside of you, and we can help you find it.

ACTIVITY: *Birthright*

Being loved is not your only birthright—there are a million and one happy, healthy, exciting things that you were born for and to. Let's start thinking of them.

Cut a piece of paper into strips. Use as many as you want. On each strip write a birthright. Start with this statement: It is my birthright to be . . .

Write as many of them as you can. Place them in a shoebox, a plastic bag, or a pillowcase. Every day, as many times a day as you wish, draw a birthright and read it out loud. Or, you can post them on your wall or on your bathroom mirror with post-its as a constant reminder of the wonder and joy and bounty you are born to have. Here are some suggestions. Feel free to use them.

It is my birthright to be loved.

It is my birthright to be respected.

It is my birthright to be safe.

It is my birthright to have good friends.

It is my birthright to have a loving and happy home.

Creating a New Story

Up until this point, most of the help you have received from a therapist or counselor or a support group has probably focused on processing the violation you experienced. The reason for this is that a lot of therapies are influenced by the idea that "what is mentionable is manageable, what is unmentionable is unmanageable." Thus, these professionals have helped you "name" the violation you endured by telling your story. This is an important part of the healing process. If you have not had a chance to tell your story, stop now and find a support group, therapist, or even a friend who can listen to you, help you put a name to what happened to you, and lend an ear for you to share your story. You need to be able to give voice to what you have gone through.

If you *have* had the chance to tell your story of violation, it is now time to create a new story. This one will focus on who you are in the face of what you have been through and who you can and will become. This is the work of reclamation and it begins by you thinking about what *new* story you can tell about yourself and your future. You already know where you have been; that story is ending. In fact, you are probably an expert on where you have been and what you have been through. Now it is time to take a look at the unknown—where you are going and how to develop new expertise to live your life free of violation. As you create this story, you will think about yourself in a new and positive way, heal your past, and imagine your future.

Embracing Thriver-Thinking

As you move through the healing process and spend more and more time in the Thriver stage, it's time to focus your attentions on developing skills for your future. During your violation, you learned a number of skills that helped you adapt, cope, and survive. We want to honor some of those life skills—after all, they got you to this point in your life. For example, you are likely very attuned to the needs of others, able and willing to please others, and able to put your own needs last.

While it's great to have something positive to take away from your violation, we now want you to develop new skills for this leg of your healing journey. These skills will enable you to envision a perfect future, claim the gifts that lie in front of you, and create a wonderful life. We call the process of developing these skills "Thriver-thinking," because it requires you to focus your energy and attention on creating a new story and future. You are quite literally developing a new way of thinking. Many of the creative exercises in this book are centered around building Thriver-thinking skills. For example, some activities utilize symbols and metaphors to help you heal while moving forward, while others challenge you to use your imagination and "think outside the box," which is an important skill for Thrivers.

What Is Thriver-Thinking?

Thriver-thinking is boundless. Thriver-thinking or the thinking you do when you are healing is different from the "Survivor-thinking" that has gotten you to this point.

- **Survivor-thinking** teaches you to hunker down, prepare for the worst, anticipate a range of consequences, and to think only of the short-term or immediate future.
- **Thriver-thinking** is expansive, limitless, and full of possibility. Thriver-thinking helps you prepare for the best, and to dream about the wonderful possibilities that belong to you and your life.

Imagination Comes Into Play

Think for a minute about the world of imaginative play. Perhaps you experienced this world as a child or witnessed imaginative play with your own children or with children you have cared for. Imaginative play allows children to create a limitless and boundless world where they are not confined by the rules of ordinary life. When you were a child you may have played games with your siblings or friends in which what you imagined was real and possible. For example, when Danielle and her sister were children they played a variation of the game "house" and traveled the world on winged ponies. You may have also experienced boundless imagination in dreams. You might fly, time may pass either faster or slower, you might know what people think even though they haven't spoken, and you can be in two places at once. This is because your imagination creates these possibilities. In your dream state or in your play as a child—these worlds really exist. They are "real."

Let's think about the creative power of the imagination in another way. In her Harry Potter series, author J. K. Rowling essentially created entirely new worlds out of blank pages of paper. The story has become a wonderful escape for many people around the world and has certainly transformed Ms. Rowling's life. Simply by using her imagination, she transformed herself from a destitute single parent to a multimillionaire who can provide anything she wants for her children. She used a type of Thiver-thinking to create a different reality for herself and her family. She imagined a different world, wrote about it, and then found a way to publish her book and change her life. Like creating a book, you are creating your own life. What you experience comes from you—you can create your world. Anything is possible! And much of it begins in the most powerful tool you possess—your imagination.

Revive Your Imagination

Most likely, as you grew up, someone told you that the world of imaginative play was impossible; "reality" was contrasted to "fantasy" and the latter was demeaned or looked down upon. You were also told that "only little kids" who did not know any better engaged in or believed in imaginative play. Maybe you were told in some pretty harsh ways to "grow up" and leave your fantasies behind. Perhaps you were told not to get your hopes up. Well here is some pretty amazing news: The skills you developed as a child to create limitless worlds are *exactly* the skills you need to create your ideal life. Unlearn the idea that reality is the opposite of fantasy and relearn how to dream. It is fantasy that leads to the reality of being a doctor, jewelry maker, writer, landscaper, actor, social worker, lawyer, or even a contortionist for Cirque du Soleil. In dreaming, you can create an image of what you most want, and using that image, devise a way to obtain it. What would have happened if J. K. Rowling had believed that a blank piece of paper was just a blank piece of paper and the only reality that existed was endless poverty? Remember our motto:

> **If you can dream it, you can see it. If you can see it, you can get there.**

A Different Kind of "What If"

Do you remember the "what ifs" that you left behind in the last unit? Well, here is a different kind of "what if" to think about. Ask yourself the following "what if" questions:

- What if my life was perfect?
- What if I had everything I wanted?
- What if I was happy? What would happiness feel like?

Just as children play in a world without limits, you can heal through metaphor and symbolic play. Retraining yourself to imagine limitless thinking can lead to sustainable life changes.

Rediscover Your Power

When you played as a child, you made the rules. The same is true now. You make the rules for this game called your life and the only obstacles you will encounter are ones that you give power to. You are a limitless being in a limitless world. You can do or be anything. Think about that for a minute. Does it sound very different from the messages you have heard all your life? Is there a voice inside your head that says, "No way. Not my life. Not me"? That's because you were told that you were powerless and you were made to feel like you were powerless. Listen to that voice and then get ready to say good-bye to it.

Now it is time to hear a new voice. Begin now. Say softly to yourself, "I am powerful. I am full of my own power. I radiate power. I can have and do anything." Say it louder now. (You can even yell if you want to!) How does that feel to say that out loud? Our guess is that there is a little voice inside you that doesn't believe it. That voice may instead point to all the rotten things that have happened in your life to make you feel powerless, helpless, and trapped. That's okay. It took a lot of time for you to lose your power; it will likewise take time to regain it. *We* know that you are power-ful. And we will hold that belief for you until you are ready and able to own it. The next time you are afraid or anxious, remind yourself of your own power. And don't be afraid to say it loudly.

Here are just a few things to consider before getting started on this meditation and on the rest of the activities in this unit.

Find Time and Space

Many women are pretty talented multitaskers. We are used to carrying a lot of weight and responsibility and doing a lot of things at once. While we may have to do this to survive, healing and thriving require making space for ourselves only.

So before you begin the following activities, do a quick inventory. Do you have some time right now for these activities? It is absolutely okay to take a block of time just for you. In fact, it is more than okay—it is really important. You'll actually take care of others well when you take care of yourself. It isn't selfish. It is vital to your healing and your ability to make the life you want for yourself and your family.

Find Energy

The energy you want to bring to the healing process is a calm, focused, and open-minded energy. While it can be difficult to slow yourself down and listen to the rhythms of your body, through practice it will get easier. Breathing and meditation can help you relax and focus your attention on you, your body, and your creative powers.

The Benefits of Meditation

The following activity is a meditation. Women healing from a violation often like meditating, even those who have never done it before. It allows you to practice using your mind for self-discovery and for the important task of creation. Where violation taught you to stay out of your body or that your body exists only for someone else's pleasure, meditation is a great way to climb back into your body, to see what a great place it is to be in, and to see how your mind and body are connected.

Even if it seems a little foreign at first, give meditation a try. With practice, you will find that you are developing new skills that allow you to succeed.

Getting Started

Follow this process as you begin any meditation. First, find a quiet place where you will not be interrupted. Make sure to turn off your music. Turn off the TV. Shut down your phone.

Now, take a minute to get comfortable. Adjust your body until you feel comfortable: Roll your shoulders, straighten your back, stretch, take off your shoes, etc.

Place your hand on your belly just below your rib cage. Take a deep breath in. Do you feel your hand rise? See if the air you take in can push your hand up.

Meditation for Healing

Even when you were in the worst moments of your violation, you kept the essence of yourself protected and safe. You needed to protect your essence, so you buried it deep inside you. It is time for this wonderful essence to come out and to be a part of your everyday life. Meditation is a great way to access this essence again in a safe and reassuring way.

ACTIVITY: *Belly-Breathing Basics*

The following meditation is designed to give you a sacred and safe way to allow your treasured self to emerge. Your treasured self is a key part of the identity you're trying to reclaim. The way we breathe is important to the way we feel, so we're first going to focus on healthy breathing techniques. To allow a feeling of comfort to seep into our bodies, we use deep, belly breaths, letting out all the used air and bringing in the new air. To belly breathe, put your hand over your bellybutton and feel your belly expand when you take air in and deflate when you push the air out.

You may have noticed that when you are scared or stressed, you take in short breaths from your chest. This type of breathing does not allow all the depleted air to leave your body, nor does it allow in the amount of fresh oxygen you need. Shallow chest breathing can add to a feeling of stress because your body must make do with stale air and becomes oxygen starved.

If you instead consciously take deep belly breaths, some of your stressed feeling may subside. The next time you feel nervous, stressed, or scared, try putting your hand on your belly and feel it expand with good air and let go of the used air. You may be surprised to find yourself feeling calmer and less scared or stressed.

ACTIVITY: *Finding Your Sacred Space and Your Word*

Find a quiet place where you will not be interrupted. Adjust your body until you feel comfortable: roll your shoulders, straighten your back, stretch, take off your shoes, etc.

The following meditation is designed to give you a sacred and safe way to allow your treasured self to emerge and to give you a word to signify that wonderful part of you that you have saved through all your experiences. Trust yourself, believe in yourself, and don't second-guess your intuition.

Let your mind travel to a soft, safe meadow filled with fragrant, waving grass. Purple, yellow, pink, red, and white flowers look so lovely among the fronds of grass and fill the air with a delicate, sweet scent. You can hear the faint song of birds. You meander on a path through the meadow. You know you are perfectly safe and cannot be harmed in this space.

You are drawn to a forest on the edge of the meadow. You feel safe as you step onto a path leading into the shade of protective old trees. Birds welcome you with their joyful songs. You stroll along the path, enjoying the cool shade of the forest, seeing the warm colors of the leaves and the tree bark.

An orange light begins to filter through the trees as the sun is setting. In this mystical orange light, between day and night, you come to a clearing in the forest. This is your clearing, your grove of trees. They stand in a protective circle around you. On the ground is a soft carpet of velvety green grass. It is perfect and inviting. This is your Sacred Space. Whatever you need is here. There may be a cottage, an inviting bench, or a flower garden. There may be a picket fence around the space or just the trees guarding the border to your space. Take a moment and see your Sacred Space. . . .

This is your space and no one else's. Only you may enter your space. No other person or being may enter this space without your permission. This is your space to come to whenever you want. It is always right here, waiting for you. Only you know the way.

You walk around your Sacred Space with a sense of pride and wonder that this perfect place is your own. At one end of your space, you notice a table with a few items on it. You are drawn to a small present wrapped in lavender tissue paper. You know it is for you because all blessings in this space are yours. You unwrap the tissue paper and find a delicate necklace with a pendant that is a small rolled piece of paper, a tiny scroll. You know that when you unroll the scroll there will be a word on it. You will read it and will trust yourself. Unroll the small scroll. What word do you see?

Remember this word. It signifies the wonderful essence of you and reminds you who you are. It is your Sacred Word. Reroll the scroll and put the necklace around your neck. The scroll dangles reassuringly, keeping your Sacred Word near your heart. It is yours to keep with you always. It will guide you on your journey and protect you from harm. You feel gratitude, love, and warmth. Through your Sacred Word, you are connected to all goodness and beauty.

Lemon-yellow light of a new day comes through the trees and you know it is time to leave your Sacred Space. But you also know your Sacred Space will be here for you whenever you want or need to be here. Look around your space one more time and take the few steps from your grove back onto your path. The light of the new day and the song of the birds surround you with joy.

You walk back the way you came along the path, out of the forest and into the morning sun in the meadow. Your step is light as you stroll across the meadow. As you approach the edge of the meadow, you begin to see your familiar surroundings again and know that you are back from your meditation journey. As you re-enter, you feel relaxed and happy. Take a moment to be back in the here and now. You bring with you your Sacred Word, your joy, and the knowledge that you have your own Sacred Space. Take a few deep breaths.

Write down your Sacred Word. What does your word mean to you? What does the word tell you about yourself? You may also want to write down your thoughts about your Sacred Word in your journal. Where does it come from? Why is it your word? What does it signify?

Now, create an affirmation using your Sacred Word. Begin this way:

I am _____.

I have always been _____.

I will always be _____.

You Can't Sell from an Empty Cart

Few people make lasting or positive life changes when they are experiencing the depths of despair, hopelessness, and desperation. To make lasting changes, you want to get in touch with an "inner self" who is positive, playful, hopeful, creative, and strong. That self helped you survive. Now that same self will help you thrive.

Here is another way of thinking about how change can be made in the Thriver stage. Danielle once visited a country antique store tucked away on a back road in Connecticut. The shop was filled with carefully selected, high-quality antiques. When she commented to the store owner about the variety of her wares, the owner simply said, "You can't sell from an empty cart." When Danielle thought about this in terms of the healing process, she realized the parallel. No one can make strides to design a future when they feel their cart is empty, that is, when they feel bad or scared.

Of course, leaving an abuser, establishing a new household, and healing from the physical and psychological wounds inflicted by an abuser are important steps for survival. Now it is time to move on to the next step and begin to design a life that is high quality, exciting, and fulfilling. In order to do this, you need to have energy to create. Your metaphorical cart must be filled.

The following activities will help you flex your imagination muscles and generate "products" for your cart. These activities will help you reclaim your identity by helping you think big and happy thoughts about you, your future, and what you might want out of life.

ACTIVITY: *Imagine That!*

This exercise forces you to think of yourself first, to use your imagination to create unlimited possibilities, and to fulfill wild dreams. Imagine that you just received $5 million that you must first spend on you and your heart's desires. After that, you can do anything you want with it. Also, no one can touch this money without your permission. What will you do with it first?

1. _____

_____

_____

2. _____

_____

_____

3. _____

_____

_____

What will you do with the rest?

_____

_____

_____

_____

_____

ACTIVITY: *Three Wishes*

The purpose of this activity is to keep you thinking big, expansive thoughts. While abuse teaches women to hunker down and think thoughts of survival, healing teaches you to draw on the wisdom of your creative mind and think of unlimited possibilities. Practice makes perfect!

For this activity, imagine that you are walking along the street and you find an old oil lamp lying in the dirt. You pick it up and dust it off. Out comes a genie and offers you three wishes. The catch: You can only wish for things that will make your life better—and you can't wish for more wishes or for money! What will you wish for and how will these wishes make your life better?

1. _____

_____

_____

2. _____

_____

_____

3. _____

_____

_____

ACTIVITY: *Party Planning*

We have described how violence is isolating. In order to survive in a violating relationship, many women have to maintain their own isolation. Unfortunately, the skills to maintain isolation have then become highly developed, and the skills to connect with others have gone by the wayside. As you heal, you need others. And yet you find that you often don't have the skills necessary to reach out and connect with others. So this activity lets you imagine what skills you will need, imagine yourself using those skills, and imagine the result as positive and joyful. This is how real change often begins—through your imagination.

For the activity, imagine that you have been reading *Joyful Magazine* and see that there is a contest. The winner receives an all-expenses-paid vacation of their choice. All you have to do to win is to plan your ideal party with people you know right now. The party must leave everyone feeling happy, loved, and supported as well as accepted and important. It is a tall order, but you feel confident you can plan just such a party. In your journal, write or draw this magnificent social event! And remember how each guest—including you—must leave feeling.

You might begin by thinking what it would look like to remove some of those walls that keep you confined, separated from others, distrustful, ready to pounce and protect. What would it be like if you felt something different? What would happen if you felt free to breathe deeply, free to relax and enjoy your life and help others do the same? Let your mind wander to the most wonderful possibilities you can imagine. And create that event.

The Importance of Self-Care in Reclaiming Your Identity

Healing from violation means feeling good physically, emotionally, mentally, and spiritually, and this means taking care of yourself. During the Survival stage, every bit of your energy—physical, emotional, mental, and spiritual—was consumed by trying to stay safe and protect yourself and those you love. There was no energy left to take care of yourself. But now, as you work on becoming a Thriver, taking care of yourself is important because it helps you reclaim your identity. Women who have worked with us say they knew they were healing when they began taking care of themselves.

Why Now?

One reason women who are healing can take time for themselves when they embrace Thriver-thinking is because their life circumstances have changed. There is a time, a place, and energy for self-care. But another more important reason has to do with how you feel about yourself. When you are a

Thriver, you believe you are worth taking care of. You learn to ignore messages that suggest you are selfish if you spend time on yourself. You begin to realize that you are worth it.

Self-care has another powerful component—competence. As you begin to take care of yourself, you discover that you have the power to take care of yourself. You no longer rely on someone else to meet your needs. You are competent and capable of taking care of yourself and of providing yourself with what you need to feel happy, relaxed, loved, fed, and well cared for. You can do it and you deserve it.

Components of Self-Care

We have identified five important dimensions to taking care of the whole you. They are:

1. Your core self, your essence
2. Your body and beauty
3. Your feelings
4. Your spiritual self
5. Your social self

In this unit, we will focus on helping you take care of your essence, your true and wonderful self. We'll take a look at the other dimensions throughout this book.

Taking Care of Your Essence

When we say "taking care of your essence," we mean developing and expressing the unique and special things about you. In other words, you want to develop or bring to the forefront those characteristics or interests that make you who you are—your identity!

Women who are violated lose sight of who they really are because in order to protect ourselves, we have to hide our feelings, quiet our voices, ignore our needs and wishes. Part of recovery means uncovering this hidden self, our true selves, so that we can continue on the life path we choose. If violation teaches us to bury certain traits, Surviving tries to teach us we may not have the time or energy to develop them. But Thriving means we can reclaim them, expand them, develop them. These buried traits might be special talents like photography, quilting, scrapbooking, writing, creating art, hiking, running, biking, or swimming. Others might be special callings like caring for animals, or patience with children. Still others might be unique personality traits such as a sense of humor or intuition.

Whoever your hidden self is, it's not lost. In fact, it is still there, just waiting to be rediscovered. Taking care of who you are involves a journey to rediscover, recognize, and understand all of who you are and will be and giving voice to it. If you have always wanted to be a photographer, go find a camera; a writer, get a notebook; if you are a cook—grab that spatula! Let's start by getting reacquainted with that wonderful woman we know you are.

ACTIVITY: *My Favorites*

In this activity we begin to reclaim pieces of your identity by asserting your favorites. Then we are going to put them into practice. As you think of your favorites, remember to ignore old feelings that tell you to put others first.

My favorite food:

_____

My favorite color:

_____

My favorite sport:

_____

My favorite pastime:

_____

_____

_____

_____

My favorite song:

_____

My favorite movie:

_____

My favorite book:

_____

My favorite smell:

_____

My favorite thing to wear:

_____

My favorite story:

_____

_____

_____

_____

_____

My favorite thing to eat:

_____

My favorite thing to cook:

_____

My favorite thing to do on Sunday morning:

_____

_____

My favorite animal:

_____

My favorite place in the world:

_____

My favorite way to spend time when I am alone:

_____

_____

_____

My favorite thing to do with my friends:

_____

_____

_____

My favorite way to wear my hair:

_____

_____

My favorite way to pamper myself:

_____

_____

Any other favorites you want to mention?

_____

_____

_____

_____

_____

What a wonderful list! Keep it handy and be ready to use it. Make sure that you do or see or smell or connect to at least one of these "favorites" every week.

ACTIVITY: *Trusting Your Truth*

You know who you are. Deep down inside, you have always known. And you have kept that knowledge of your true and real self safe and protected, despite all you've been through. Make a list of words that describe the "real you," the person you really are. This might not be the self you put out there for others to see or the self who enters relationships with men. This is the self that looks out from your soul. It is the powerful you. It is the perfect you. It's important to rediscover these specific characteristics so you can reconnect with that self in the light of day, celebrate that perfect you, and rebuild your identity.

What words might you use to describe this perfect you?

I am:

1. _____
2. _____
3. _____
4. _____
5. _____
6. _____
7. _____
8. _____
9. _____

Now, choose as many of these characteristics as you want to and write an affirmation to yourself based on each characteristic. Put them in a place where you can read them every day. Some affirmations for the word "funny" might be: *I am*

funny. I make people laugh. I am fun to be around. People like
me. People like laughing with me. I like laughing with people.

When you are trying to reclaim yourself, you have to basically start from the beginning. One way to begin is to ask yourself, *Who am I and what do I hold really dear?* You probably know what your violator held dear, what he valued, and what he wanted. But what you want and value may be a little harder to grasp right now. Don't worry. It won't always be so. Once you get reacquainted with your own values, you can begin to think about how they intersect your interests and how both can be a part of your future life. In this activity, think about some of the things you really believe in; things that are such an important part of you that you wouldn't be you without them!

Take a look at the following list of values to get you thinking. Add any other values to the list you wish. After you have added all that you can think of, go through the list and check ten values that are most important to you.

- ❏ Belonging
- ❏ Calling My Own Shots
- ❏ Compassion
- ❏ Education
- ❏ Excitement
- ❏ Fairness
- ❏ Faith
- ❏ Fame
- ❏ Family
- ❏ Financial Security
- ❏ Friendship
- ❏ Happiness
- ❏ Hard Work
- ❏ Honesty
- ❏ Hospitality

- ❏ Influence
- ❏ Integrity
- ❏ Justice
- ❏ Love
- ❏ Order
- ❏ Power
- ❏ Recognition
- ❏ Respect
- ❏ Responsibility
- ❏ Self-Control
- ❏ Service to Others
- ❏ Status
- ❏ Success
- ❏ Wealth
- ❏ Working with Others

What other values might you add?

_____

_____

_____

_____

_____

_____

_____

Take a good look at the ten values you checked. Circle five of them that are more important than the others. After you have done that, try to reduce your list to three that really stand out for you. Reducing your list of values doesn't mean you are giving up any of your values. It just means you are fleshing out those that are really important to you. As you do this activity, trust your gut.

Write your three top values here:

1. _____
2. _____
3. _____

When you have finished, look at the three words that remain. Congratulations! You have just discovered three important life values. This gives you a good start for building a life direction because values and interests often intersect. For example, one of Karen's and Danielle's important values was education. Learning that led us to our teaching jobs.

ACTIVITY: *Integrating Your Values Into Your Life*

Think about your top three values and how they might intersect with your interests. Those connections can help you bring those values into your life. For example, if love is an important value for you, how would you like to have love in your life? Would this include children or a partner or a pet? If respect is an important value, how would you like to have respect in your life? Would this be the respect of your friends or the respect of your coworkers? If it is respect, how might you go about getting it?

Write a sentence about each of the three values you identified, stating how you would like that value to appear in your life. For example, your might write something like this for the value "love": I would like to have a loving family that includes a husband, two children, and a dog.

1. _____

_____

_____

2. _____

_____

_____

3. _____

_____

_____

ACTIVITY: *Advice Column*

In this next activity let's take stock of and voice what you have learned through your journey thus far. Sometimes teaching someone else is the best way to remind yourself what you already know! The point of this exercise is to express confidence in yourself and your abilities, and to outline the general path we all need to take to heal. Also, it reminds you to be as nice to yourself as you would be to the woman whose letter you're answering! Pretend that you have recently been hired by a leading newspaper as an advice columnist. You give people advice about their love lives and help them out of tough situations. Recently, you got this letter in your mailbox. How would you respond?

Dear Advice Column,
I have recently left my partner of many years. While I know he loved me and I know he needed me, he always treated me badly. I finally got the courage to leave him. But I feel so lost and alone. Can you give me some advice that might make the road ahead easier?

_____

_____

_____

_____

_____

_____

_____

_____

_____

_____

ACTIVITY: *Write Some Letters!*

Sometimes it helps to get your thoughts down on paper. This letter-writing exercise is one way to do that. It helps to be as specific as you can when you are writing these letters because it will help you get that vision for your future solidly in view. The more solid that vision is, the more you're connecting with your identity.

Hopes

Write a letter to yourself. What are you hoping for? What do you want to change? Think of it as you giving yourself some coaching. Here is how it starts:

Dear _____,

I have so many things I am hoping for right now. There are so many things I want to be different. Here are some of them. . . .

_____

_____

_____

_____

_____

_____

_____

_____

The Future You

This second letter is written from you, five years in the future, to you right now. Imagine where you are five years in the future and what your future self would share with you.

Dear _____,

Five years have passed since we began this journey. So many wonderful things have happened for us. I have so much I want to tell you!

_____

_____

_____

_____

_____

_____

_____

_____

The Happiest You

This third letter is written from the happiest you, the you filled with joy and love and gratitude. It begins like this.

Dear _____,

I am the voice of joy and love and gratitude that you have carefully kept safe and sound protected within you. In spite of all you have been through, you have kept me safe and alive. I am coming out now and I have so much I want to share with you. . . .

_____

_____

_____

_____

_____

_____

_____

_____

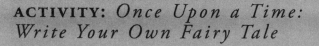

ACTIVITY: *Once Upon a Time: Write Your Own Fairy Tale*

It is time to reclaim your power as part of rebuilding your identity. You may be used to someone else calling the shots or, in effect, writing the story that you enact. This is a passive position to be in, since all you really get to do is to be a character in someone else's drama. This may be a *familiar* place to be, but it is not a *powerful* place to be.

It is time to write your own story, to reclaim your power. You began to author your own story the moment you got away from your abuser. You have the skills you need to do this already. You just need some practice.

In this activity, you will create a fairy tale. Include the following:

1. A beginning, middle, and ending point
2. A main character who is a woman
3. A main character who goes through hardship and learns some valuable life lessons

You may want to write this story. Or you may want to draw pictures or make a collage to illustrate the journey. You decide. Have fun and create the fairy tale you always wanted to read! Begin the way all good fairy tales begin:

Once upon a time . . .

_____

_____

_____

_____

_____

_____

_____

_____

_____

ACTIVITY: *See Me Brochure*

A brochure can serve as an advertising tool or simply serve as an informational guide. In this activity, you're going to create a brochure about you.

First, make a list of several of your most positive attributes. You might want to organize them this way: my greatest accomplishment, my best feature, my proudest moment, my favorite activity, something I'm good at.

_____

_____

_____

_____

_____

_____

_____

Next, take a piece of plain paper and fold it into thirds so it resembles a brochure. Decorate the front of your brochure however you choose. Inside, list, draw, or illustrate your wonderfulness!

ACTIVITY: *Elevator Speech*

An "elevator speech" is a quick speech that provides a lot of information to someone in a very short amount of time. It is designed to get someone's attention and to convey the most important or essential part of an issue or idea very quickly. Let's try it with you.

Write a "thirty-second elevator speech" explaining the most important values and beliefs that will help you live the life you desire. Make sure you include the following:

- Your wonderful qualities
- Your beliefs and values
- Your goals for the future
- Your plan for the future

For example: "Hi, I am (your name) and I'm an adventurous, courageous, and loving woman. One of my most important goals is to live a life full of gratitude. I have always been envious of those who can naturally see the best in each and every person they encounter, and can just genuinely appreciate life. Therefore, I will make a concerted effort to take five minutes each day to express my appreciation for the beautiful world in which I live. I will breathe in the fresh Montana air, I will laugh, I will love, I will seek out peace each and every day." Now it is your turn. Tell us about you!

_____

_____

_____

_____

_____

_____

_____

_____

_____

_____

A Time to Reflect

Reflection on the steps we take toward Thriving is important. By frequently taking stock of the changes you are making, you can be mindful of the changes that intentionally come from you and are becoming a part of you. You call the shots for this leg of your life journey. Though you want to focus on moving forward, stopping to look at the progress you've made is a great way to celebrate your successes and identify your next steps.

Reflecting on the changes you have made so far is an important step in recognizing those thoughts and beliefs that are new to you. It also helps as a benchmark on your journey.

ACTIVITY: *Reflecting*

Think back on the activities you completed in this unit to discover which has been the most helpful for you. Can you put into words why it was helpful? Recognizing what helped you make important changes means that you can focus on that piece to help you make future changes. You might also reflect on the transformation you have experienced in your life right now and celebrate it.

What has changed for you?

_____

_____

_____

_____

What new picture or image of yourself is emerging?

_____

_____

_____

_____

How have your thoughts changed?

_____

_____

_____

_____

What has changed in your living, work, or family environment? For example, did you get a job? Do you have a new place to live?

_____

_____

_____

_____

What activities do you want to repeat and why?

_____

_____

_____

_____

Which activity taught you the most about yourself?

_____

_____

_____

_____

How might you celebrate or mark the changes you've made so far?

_____

_____

_____

_____

Reclaim Your Life Path

"Though no one can go back and make a brand new start, anyone can start from now and make a brand new ending."
—Carl Bard

In this unit, you will:

- Dream up a new life direction
- Learn how to ask for what you want
- Stop negative thoughts that stymie your life path
- Work on taking care of yourself and feeling like you deserve it

Finding Your Life Path Again

Take another look at the quote that opens this unit. It basically says, you cannot change the past, but you can author your future. As a woman we worked with once said, "Never let your past hold your future hostage." You can choose your life path based on the boundless possibilities you now know are open to you.

Do you remember the "what ifs" you listed in Unit 2? They were sad "what ifs" and they involved the kind of thinking that held you in place in an abusive relationship because they were based on a reality you neither created nor controlled. We hope you now see how unhealthy those "what ifs" were.

The following activity also involves "what ifs," but a more positive kind that will help you re-create your life path. These "what ifs" are joyful, and they lead to the kind of thinking you need to reclaim your path. These "what ifs" belong to you because they are about you.

ACTIVITY: *What If . . .*

Write down your thoughts to the following questions.

What if I knew I was going to succeed? I would . . .

_____

_____

_____

_____

_____

_____

What if I had no fear? I would . . .

_____

_____

_____

_____

_____

_____

What if I had a magic wand? I would . . .

_____

_____

_____

_____

_____

_____

Imagination and the Law of Attraction

Remember the motto we mentioned in the introduction? "If you can dream it, you can see it. If you can see it, you can get there." This goal means that you're able to flesh out your goals so you know where you are going. It also has to do with something called the Law of Positive Attraction. Knowing something, seeing it, visualizing it, and desiring it are ways of attracting your goals to you.

The Role of Energy in Reclaiming Your Life Path
Energy is encapsulated in our bodies and released in our actions, thoughts, interactions, and relationships. Therefore,

we can think of people and the universe as being energy driven. Your goal is to identify and attract the right kind of energy into your life.

Think for a minute about how you may have experienced different kinds of energy around you. Have you ever walked into a room and sensed a person's gloomy or angry mood? You can feel the energy that angry people radiate before they ever say a word. You can feel it in their mood, their facial expressions, their body language. They create anger in others, attract other angry people to them, and attract events that will maintain or fuel their anger. This is a perfect example of energy and the law of attraction; the energy that a person is putting out is the energy he or she is getting back.

Other emotions work in the same way. Those who are depressed speak in eclipsed, monotone sentences that are received and parroted back to them by people they talk to. Someone who is cheerful and joyful is able to share that energy back and forth between someone she's talking to. Have you ever been drawn to people who radiate positive energy? When you are around them you feel happy, hopeful, and peaceful? Chances are, you are picking up on their energy, and it is affecting your own energy for the better, literally changing your outlook.

A Positive Outlook Brings You Good Things

Have you ever thought, *Boy, some people are so lucky, they have everything?* Well, guess what? You are lucky too. Just like angry and mean people can attract like energy from the universe to fuel their rage, happy and positive people can and do attract wonderful things to fuel their joy. Chances are, this is a skill that you have always had, but it was buried during your unhealthy relationship. Now is the time to become familiar with it for the first time or relearn it as a way of reclaiming your life path.

The Law of Positive Attraction is the idea that energy attracts like energy. Through the energy you send into the universe, you create the world around you by attracting a similar energy. This is very good news indeed. Because when you put out happy, grateful, well-loved energy—guess what comes back to you? This means that you are in control of what happens to you. Think about how different that is from the reality you lived with when you were in an abusive relationship. Your violator may have controlled your life, but those days are done. You control it now. And one of the ways you do this is by understanding that you can attract what you wish for by focusing your energy in a particular way.

. . . Just Like a Negative Outlook Brings You Bad Things

This is good news, but it should come with a warning, too. If you focus on your shortcomings, failures, anger, disappointment, and problems, you are putting out a very particular type of energy that will attract events, occurrences, and people with similar energy. For example, if you obsess over what you lack and use language that reflects that lack (*I don't have a good place to live; I hate my neighborhood; I need a job*)—guess what you get? More lack, want, hate, need.

Does that mean that if bad things happen, you didn't think enough good thoughts? Probably not. Sometimes bad things happen to really nice people. Theologians have been wrestling with why for eons. Here is our take: Sometimes bad things just happen. The good news is that you can choose how to respond to them, and the way you respond can turn them around. Through thought, your imagination, and active daydreaming, you have the power to create. So create wonderful things and attract them to you. To do that, you must pay attention to your thoughts, the energy your thoughts create, your vibrations, your language, and what you want to attract. You must be aware of the energy you feel and the energy you put out into the universe. Similar to the triangle with your body, mind, and feelings, you can think of another triangle that includes your reality, energy, and self.

So Focus on the Good!

It is important to develop patterns of positive thinking and acting premised on recognizing the goodness and perfection around you. By emitting positive energy in the form of direct, clear, positive goals, you can attract positive things in your life. They might be small, like a smile that is returned to you, or really, really big, like a great place to live, a wonderful job, and a great loving relationship.

You have the power. You are the author of your own future. That positive energy shapes your sense of self and creates the life path that you want.

Psychic Self-Defense: Stay Away from Those Joy-Stealers

Learning to create positive energy is like any other new skill—you will need to practice to become good at it. Here are some tips and tricks to remember as you encounter the ups and downs of any learning process. We call this psychic self-defense.

1. **Think differently about yourself and the world around you.** You no longer have to take a defensive stance to people or situations. Remember, you are in charge. You are in control. You are driving this train. So instead of reacting to a threat or lack of something (money, job, home), try acting positively, calmly, surely in a world of abundance, generation, and perfection. See that world. Live there.

2. **Protect your positive thoughts and feelings from any harm or negativity.** By protecting your thoughts and feelings, you maintain a positive energy and actually contribute to changing the energy around you. Later in this unit, you'll see a meditation for shielding that we have found very effective. Just as you would not step into a building filled with toxic smoke without a gas mask, you would not want to wade into a pit of negative energy without also being shielded by a strong defense system.

3. **Find some ways to let negative energy pass by you and not "stick" to you.** Only invest in positive energy. Don't hold on to the other stuff. Breathe out anxiety. Breathe in smiles. Breathe out worry. Breathe in fluffy clouds. Breathe out anger and fear. Breathe in pink cake. There are people in everyone's life who really make them mad or in some

way push their buttons. Your life is no exception. Remember, you can't control other people or their behavior. If you tried you probably only got frustrated. But you can control yourself. You can control how you behave and what you feel. If you let other people make you mad or frustrated, then you have let them spread their negative energy to you. And you have invested in their negative energy. You have a choice about this. Let their negative energy pass right over you. Don't even recognize it. This takes practice (meditation can help!), but as you feel better about yourself and your own life path, it gets easier to do.

4. **Change the energy around you by changing the company you keep.** If you keep company with people whose energy level is negative, chances are, you will find it difficult to maintain positive energy yourself. Take a mental inventory to spot where and what might need to change. To spot "energy leaks," ask yourself these questions:

- Are you in a living situation where you feel supported and nurtured?
- Are you in a living situation where you can be positive about your life?
- Are you in a living situation where you feel safe from harm?
- Are you around nice people during the day and the evening?
- Are you around people who say nice things to you?
- Are you around people who see how wonderful you are?
- Are you around people who smile and laugh?
- Are you around people who say kind things about others?

- Are you around people who understand where you are going?
- Are you around people who think you are good and worthy?
- Are you around people who make you feel happy and loved?
- Are you in a living or work situation where you can laugh every day?

If you answered yes to these questions, you are keeping good company! If you answered no to some or the majority of them, you may want to think about changing your living or work environment. If you cannot change either of those at this time, then you really need to learn to deflect negative energy until you can make a change, and then, you will want to manifest a change.

ACTIVITY: *Meditations for Protection*

Here are two meditations that you can read to yourself. Both of them deal with protection—meaning, surrounding yourself with protective energy when you encounter people whose energy is not positive or if you encounter someone who is a joy-stealer.

Protective Light and Mother Earth

Relax. Breathe in. Breathe out. Breathe in. Breathe out.

Read this to yourself: Mother Earth nurtures us, protects us, and loves us. We are connected with Earth through the food we eat, the air we breathe, and the houses we live in upon her surface. Every day, we walk upon the earth. We are born onto this planet and when we die we go back into the planet and become a part of Mother Earth once again.

Feel your connection with Earth. Feel your feet solidly on the planet. Let roots grow out of your feet and down into the soft rich dirt of Mother Earth. Let your roots grow deeper and deeper into the center of the earth. As your roots grow down into the center of the earth, you are surprised to find a pool of white light at its core. Your roots delve into the white light pool and soak up the white light, which moves up through your roots and into your body.

This is strong protective white light. The protective white light reaches your feet, moves into your legs, your thighs, your torso, your chest, your shoulders, your head, and now surrounds you completely. You have protective white light all around you and you feel comfort in the protection. Your protective white light lets in only that which is in your highest and best interest.

You are safe. You are protected. You can keep protective white light around you all the time. When you feel scared, reinforce your protective light by bringing more up from the earth. There is an unlimited supply of protective light and it is always available to you.

Let your roots come back into your feet and feel yourself solidly on planet Earth. Keep your protective white light around you.

Protection: Eggshell of White Light

Relax. Breathe in. Breathe out. Breathe in. Breathe out.

Read this to yourself: Imagine that you are enveloped by a protective eggshell of white light. It begins at your head and swoops down the front of your body, slips under your feet and travels up the back side of you to join where it began. It covers your entire body. You can see through it perfectly. You can move around without limitations. Your eggshell surrounds you and envelops you. And in it you know you are protected from all harm. To create the eggshell simply say:

"I am surrounded by white light. I am protected by white light. An eggshell of white light surrounds me." As you say these words see the white light form the eggshell around you. You are safe.

Use this protection whenever you feel threatened or need to change the energy in a situation, or to protect yourself against someone else's negative energy.

Stopping Negative Thoughts

Just as "catching" other people's negative thoughts can bring you down, you can also be disempowered by your own undercutting thoughts. When you first read about dreaming big to imagine your ideal life—what was your reaction? Was it fear? Did you think, "That is so unrealistic," or "I don't want to do that," or "I can't do that"? Did you feel yourself shy away from even imagining it?

Dreaming involves taking a risk. It involves hoping and believing in possibilities. Along with these possibilities comes the fear of disappointment, that you won't be able to attain your ideal life. This fear of disappointment can feel like a knot in your stomach, a tightening in your chest, or an all-body tensing reaction. It is okay to have this fear. It is natural.

Recognize it for what it is (the loss of personal power that you've experienced), understand it, sympathize with it, nurture it. But know that it is not something you should keep.

Stop!

When you find yourself dealing with doubts, "I can'ts," and other negative self-talk, you need to take protective measures, just as you did with deflecting negative energy around you. One technique is to think of a mental STOP sign in your mind when you begin to undercut your dreams with negative "what ifs" or when you begin to discredit your visions.

It is especially important for women who have been violated to pay attention to the negative internal messages or internal dialogue that plays in their heads. Many experts suggest that women who have been violated often hear the voice of a parent or a partner or a sibling in their heads as a constant negative or self-critical "chatter." These negative thoughts about your self-worth are like bathroom wallpaper. You see it, but it is so frequent or common that you absorb it without taking notice of it.

It's now time to take notice of it. Whose voice is in your head? Is this the voice of a parent who abused you or who was a harsh critic or judge? Is it the voice of the violator? Does this voice belittle you or judge you or call you names? Does this voice want to make sure you know how awful you are? Take notice of this voice and get rid of it. Think of it as an uninvited guest and change the message it plays about who you are. You know how wonderful you are, and so do a lot of other people who represent positive influences in your life. It is time to let that knowledge gain power and fill mental space. And it is time to silence the negative voice by uninviting it!

ACTIVITY: *Interrupting Your Negative Thoughts*

This activity is similar to the one we asked you to do in Unit 2, when we asked you to list the sad "what ifs." Sometimes writing down negative thoughts helps us see them for what they are and allows us to say good-bye a little more easily.

Below, list all the negative statements that play inside your head. Then see red—the red stop sign, that is. Use that mental stop sign as a way to challenge that voice's right to be in your head.

Next, you'll create a TRUTH statement based on the true you, the real you. Each time you answer one of these negative thoughts, think of a countering statement that proves it wrong. Finally, create a new and affirming voice.

Here is an example:

Negative Voice Says:	STOP	Positive Voice Says:
You're so stupid.	STOP. Ask yourself: Whose voice is that? Do you want that person and their voice in your head anymore? You get to decide.	I am not stupid. I am very smart. (Image: me receiving my high school diploma; Image: the time my teacher told me no one else got an "A" on the test but me.) Offer a replacement: I am so smart!!!

Negative Voice Says:	STOP	Positive Voice Says:
You're a bad mother.	STOP. Ask yourself: Whose voice is that? Do you want that person and their voice in your head anymore? You get to decide.	I am a great mother. I love my children and they love me. (Image: the time we went to the movies and laughed together.) Offer a replacement: I am a loving mother!

Keep in mind that you don't have to explain, justify, or excuse anything about you. Just stop that negative voice and replace it with your truth.

When you're done, turn those replacement statements into affirmations. For example, "I am smart!" or "I am successful." Write your affirmations on sticky notes and put them on your doors, bathroom mirror, dashboard—any place you will see them every day. Remind yourself of all your truths!

ACTIVITY: *Your Good Qualities*

In order to allow a new voice in your head, it will be important to get lots of practice. You've heard plenty of negative voices, so it's time to start a chorus of positive ones. This activity gives you practice. It is time to remind yourself what a wonderful person you are. Use these prompts to bring your great qualities to the forefront of your mind.

Wonderful things about me:

_____

_____

Things I do really well:

_____

_____

Wonderful qualities I have:

_____

_____

I like myself because:

_____

_____

I am proud of myself because:

_____

_____

ACTIVITY: *A Brand New Way to Talk to Yourself*

Chances are good that just as there were people in your life who helped fuel your negative self-talk, you know people who have seen your gifts, who know your talents, and who see you for the wonderful person you are. These voices of encouragement and strength become part of you when you can acknowledge that you did something courageous or kind or when you are successful. It can be beneficial as you chart your new life path to think of these voices as a helpful chorus cheering you on and acknowledging how proud they are of you. When you held on to the negative, critical voices that played in your head, you were, in a sense, cataloguing them, pulling them out to further remind yourself of your shortcomings when things did not go well for you. Well, now it's time to catalogue the positive statements and consciously pull them out whenever you like.

Think about any positive things that people have said about you. These might be a trusted friend, a coworker, a therapist or counselor, or even your third-grade teacher! Start making a list or recording them on index cards. They might read like this, "You are smart." "You are the only friend I ever had." "You cared about me." "You are so funny." "You care about your kids." Next, think about the positive things you stated about yourself in the previous activity. Now add some comments from you to your list or index cards.

Now, you can make positive self-talk statements that you can practice repeating when you need a boost. Take a look at the examples. These new messages can play when things are going well and when things go wrong.

My New Self-Talk:

1. I am wonderful!
2. I don't have to be perfect to be a good person.
3. I made a mistake—and I learned something new!

Now you try. . . .

1. _____

2. _____

3. _____

Dreaming Up a New Life Path

How do you imagine a life path for yourself, now that you're free of your violation? The answer is by dreaming, creating, and expanding your vision of what is possible. To do so you must involve your body, your thoughts, and your feelings. While violation kept you small, constricted, and defensive, dreaming or envisioning allows you to invest in a universe that is boundless, and full of wonder, magnificence, and possibility. Dreaming asks you to reject all of the old rules you learned through violation and create new rules to thrive by. Dreaming allows you to create reality, because as you dream, you create both a vision and a positive, creative, hope-filled energy. This energy manifests in the physical world through actions, events, outcomes, and people you meet and draw to yourself. As you reclaim your power and identity, you will also reclaim your ability to dream and plan the life you want for yourself.

Daytime Dreaming

The kind of dreaming we are talking about happens when you are awake. This dreaming happens when you let your imagination wander and explore the marvelous "what ifs" rather than the potential terrible ones. You probably have some practice in the kind of disaster "dreaming" that produces buckets of worrisome, anxiety-based, negative energy. This is a new practice and it is important. The work of Rick Hanson, a neuropsychologist (*www.rickhanson.net*) shows that positive dreaming like that achieved through meditation or by intentionally focusing our attention on positive experiences and feelings can increase positive signals in the brain while reducing negative ones and actually change the physiology of the brain. This contributes to improved health and a positive sense of well-being. Another way to think about dreaming is by comparing it to glasses or contact lenses. Most people who wear glasses see the world very differently with their glasses on than with them off. What if the lens you put on in the morning, instead of helping you see better close up or far away, actually helped you see things more positively? How would you conduct your day if everything you saw was wonderful, beautiful, peaceful, supportive, loving? You have worn the lens of violation and subjugation, and you responded without even thinking about it; you acted in response to your experiences. Now you must train your brain to see and respond to different truths. As you see different truths and respond to them, you will create them for yourself in the material world.

What to Dream About

Start by daring to dream about your perfect life, your perfect partner, your perfect home, your perfect job, your perfect haircut, your perfect shoes, your perfect outfit, your perfect body. Do not get caught up in thinking your dreams are not realistic; the point of dreaming is to create a new reality where anything can happen. Go ahead and dream big, fantastic dreams. When you dream, pay attention to your feelings and to the energy these visions create for you—they're likely happy, invigorating, and motivating. You will learn how to hold on to these feelings. Trust them. Expand upon them. Dreaming like this helps you build a life that is boundless, happy, spontaneous, and self-fulfilling.

So what would happen if you engaged in the kind of thinking that is magical, unlimited, and full of joy? Try thinking about "what if" statements like the following. While you think about them, consider what happens next. To do this, end each sentence with "and." Now you try.

- What if I lived happily ever after?
- What if I won the lottery and bought a house?
- What if I colored my hair pink and it looked great?

- What if I bumped into someone today who said I looked fabulous and . . .
- What if I smiled at a stranger and the stranger smiled back and . . .
- What if I had a great day and . . .
- What if I had everything I needed and . . .
- What if I painted my apartment walls green and pink and lavender and . . .
- What if my car did not die and instead ran for another thousand miles and . . .
- What if I smelled something so wonderful I went back and smelled it again and . . .
- What if I got a break today and . . .

When Negative Thoughts Intrude

As you learn to develop positive dreaming abilities, you will find that negative disaster thinking may intrude on your thoughts. When that happens, pull out that mental STOP sign. Pay attention to yourself and your inner thoughts so you can STOP negative thinking and turn it around the moment it starts.

Every time you start to see the negative or the disasters that can happen to stop your positive "what ifs," stop yourself. Remind yourself of your gratitude list. Remind yourself of the wonderful things to which you are entitled. See your life and yourself as perfect. Don't be surprised if this is a skill, like any other, that you have to practice. Don't be surprised if it takes time to adjust your thinking. You have had a lot of practice seeing what you need and what you don't have. It will take practice seeing what you wish to bring into your life and holding that in your gaze until it arrives. So this isn't you waiting for good things to happen to you. This is you actively bringing them to you by using one of the most powerful muscles in your body, your brain, and your imagination.

ACTIVITY: *My Perfect Life Starts Now*

Here are two activities to get you started thinking about all the wonderful, miraculous things that lie ahead for you.

Activity: My Ideal Day

Write down what your ideal day would look like from start to finish. Include specifics like who you see, where you live, what you eat, and what you do from the moment you wake up to the moment you fall asleep. If you're feeling creative, you can draw or make a collage to illustrate your day. The more clearly you see this day—the better!

Activity: My Ideal Life

Now that you've imagined a wonderful *day*, build that into a wonderful *life.* What more general themes do you see when you imagine your perfect life?

_____

_____

_____

_____

_____

_____

_____

_____

_____

_____

_____

_____

ACTIVITY: *How Did Your Ideal Life Make You Feel?*

Now that you imagined your ideal day and life, it's time to capture the emotions and feelings that exercise elicited. You can learn to invite these emotions back and create a life path that allows them to flourish.

What specific emotions did you feel as you thought about your ideal life?

How can you hold on to these feelings this week?

What would happen if you lived your life as if it were perfect?

Create some affirmations that will help this perfect life manifest in your life. Begin with these prompts:

I will . . .

_____

_____

_____

I have . . .

_____

_____

_____

I am . . .

_____

_____

I know . . .

_____

_____

_____

Language and the Power to Ask

Many women have been taught how to be a "proper woman," or how to be a "good girl," whether by parents, teachers, or society. Qualities that make a "proper woman" may not seem bad at first glance:

- Be polite
- Take care of your own needs; don't ask for help
- Be concerned about other's needs above your own; put yourself last
- Endure hardship rather than complain about it

If these messages sound like any part of your upbringing, then you share a great deal in common with a lot of women. The problem is, those skills are not helpful to you as you build a new life post-violation. You may have even internalized them to an extreme, unhealthy degree. Now, you need to *put yourself first*. You need to *ask for help* and *make claims* to what you want. You need to *fix problems* rather than endure them.

To do those things, it is important to develop or sharpen some language skills to be able to communicate your feelings and needs. These skills may change the way you have thought about what a woman is and should be.

The Power of Asking

Asking for what you want may seem aggressive or impolite to you at first. Or, you may have thought that asking for something—furniture, clothes, food, shelter—put you in a powerless situation. You believed that you had to give up your power to ask for something. What if you held on to your power and asked?

Although it's acceptable for men to ask for what they want and negotiate for a better deal, girls and women in our society have been trained to accept what they get. They are encouraged to take what they're given and to shy away from negotiating for a better situation for themselves.

Bear in mind: It is not just you and it is not just women who have experienced violation who act this way. In a study by Linda Babcock, professor of economics at Carnegie Mellon University, all graduating professional school students were advised to negotiate their starting salaries. Fifty-seven percent of the men but only 7 percent of the women negotiated their starting salaries. On average, those who negotiated increased their initial compensation by just over 7 percent, which was approximately $10,000 per year more than those who did not negotiate. That's a big difference in yearly salary, and the difference grows when yearly raises are based on the initial salary. Assuming a 3 percent raise per year, that adds up to $600,000 more over the course of a career just for asking for more compensation at the initial offer. Yet only *7 percent* of women asked. They gave up their power and accepted what they were given. You need to learn to ask.

Examples of Asking for What You Want

Begin with the image that the universe is filled with abundance and you can simply scoop up what you need—like dipping a ladle into a flowing stream. Holding the ladle gives you power! Dipping into a stream of endless possibilities is also a powerful way to think about all the wonderful things that are available to you.

What about the feeling that you're being impolite or aggressive? Let it go. You are simply asking for what you deserve—your ideal life.

Here's a simple example of asking for what you want. Whenever we check into hotels and are told the room rate, we each smile and look the clerk in the eye and say, "I would like to pay less than that." Sometimes we smile and might say, "I don't want to pay that." We always begin with an "I" statement and express our individual truth. We only express the truth we experience. We keep it positive and express our intention. Instead of saying, "That is too much for a room," or "You are charging too much" (that's someone else's reality that we simply cannot know or judge) or "I can't afford that!" (which creates a reality you do not want to invite into your life), we just state an intention. "I would like to pay less than that."

Our results? Well, sometimes there is not much wiggle room based on market demands beyond our control and we do pay the full price for a room. But most of the time, we pay much less. Part of reclaiming your power is to learn to ask directly for the things you want from others—without blaming others for failing to provide things for you; without making excuses for yourself, your inabilities, or your needs; and without feeling badly or shameful. Let it go. Blaming, excuses, and bad feelings are from the past. You have power now and you are simply going to ask, in a straightforward and direct way, for what you need and want.

Danielle met a woman in one of her groups who experienced a loss of a beloved family member. She wanted to honor that relative by creating a memorial in her home consisting of a candle and a special plant that he had loved. When she went to the florist to purchase the plant, she saw that it was way more money than she had. Using power language, she stood up nice and tall, she took some deep calming breaths, looked the clerk in the eyes, smiled, and very respectfully said, "I would like to pay half price for this plant." Guess what happened? She got the plant for half price. She was able to create a memorial and in her own way, say good-bye to her relative.

Tips That Work

As you practice asking for what you want, think about these techniques:

- Check your body posture. Hold you head high, look people directly in the eyes, smile if it seems appropriate.
- Begin with an "I" statement that is *not* followed by the words "need," "don't have," or "want." Instead, make it positive. There is no place for anger, guilt, manipulation, cajoling, pleading, or begging. No justification of your needs is necessary. In our example earlier, the woman did not say, "I need this plant for my memorial." That would have created need. That would also have placed her in a powerless position of asking for something she didn't really believe she deserved. Instead, she kept it positive and affirmative.
- Accept that you have needs and also accept that you have a right to have your needs fulfilled and gratified. Start small.
  "I would like some coffee, please."
  "I would like to pay less for those shoes."
  "I would like bus fare, please"
  "I would like to go home now."
  "I would like to have full custody of my children."
  "I would like to work for you. And I would like more money than you are currently offering."
- It also helps to be very clear about what you want and to keep that vision in your mind as you ask. When you are unclear about what you want, you can't be clear with others. Let's put these skills into practice.

ACTIVITY: *What Would You Like?*

Think for a minute about your life. What would you like to attract? How can you phrase that in a powerful and positive way? In your journal, begin with this writing prompt:

"I would like . . ." or "I will attract into my life . . ."

Make a list and make it as specific as possible. Write down those statements.

_____

_____

_____

_____

_____

_____

_____

_____

_____

_____

_____

ACTIVITY: *Active vs. Passive Voice*

Women have also been trained to use passive words and sentence structures. Here are some examples of how some women talk passively and how they could talk more powerfully. Fill in your own statements in the blank columns. Identify some ways you have of asking that are passive and turn them into active/power statements or requests.

Passive	Active
Is it all right with you if I meet my friends tonight?	I am meeting my friends tonight.
Would you like to stop and get some coffee?	I would like some coffee.
I sort of tend to think . . .	I believe . . .
I'm really busy and I don't want to . . . but I'll find the time.	No, sorry. I won't.
If only I had . . .	Starting now, I will.
You'll have to excuse my . . .	Nothing! (Don't make excuses!)

As you identify some of the passive ways you use language, practice ways you would change these statements with someone. Practicing with someone can help make the activity more real, like a dress rehearsal, and a pal can give you immediate feedback about how you did. Don't be surprised if you laugh a lot! If you do not have a group of women to practice with, grab your daughter or a female friend and practice together. Have fun!

ACTIVITY: *Use Powerful Language*

In this activity, you are going to work on using language that is powerful, direct, and positive to create requests. You will practice asking for things using clear, direct language that simply asserts what it is you need or want.

Here are some rules:

1. Sorry! No excuses or justifications accepted. Keep explanations to a minimum. No begging, pleading, or groveling, either!

2. Focus on what you want. If you want a job, then ask: "I would like this job." If you want to pay your rent a week late with no penalty, then ask: "I would like to pay my rent this month on October 15th and incur no penalty." If you are looking for a wonderful new apartment or looking to get summer camp for your kids paid for, power language can help. Start by writing or thinking, "I would like . . ." The only word you can't use after "like" is a word that points to someone else. You are only asking for yourself in this activity!

3. Imagine the person in your head to whom you are making the request; then write your request.

4. After you write your requests, turn to the person you are practicing with and look her directly in the eyes. Pretend you are looking at the person to whom you will make the request.

5. Hold you head up high, keep your back straight, and throw your shoulders back! Take several calming breaths. Concentrate on the outcome.

Get a pleasant expression on your face and make your request!!

I would like . . .

_____

_____

_____

_____

_____

_____

_____

I would like . . .

_____

_____

_____

_____

_____

_____

Well, how was it? You might feel silly at first, but keep at it. Try this exercise several times each week. Get good at holding on to your power and simply asking for what you need.

Reminder: when making your requests, do not use words like "want" and "need." For example, "I need a new pair of shoes." The reason for this is that need and want are deficit terms. They signify things we don't have. If you put this type of energy out—guess what you get back? Deficit—want and need. Use only power language that is positive, affirmative, and that points directly to what it is you wish to attract.

The Importance of Self-Care: Taking Care of Your Body and Beauty

In Healing Unit 3, we introduced the idea that there are five ways women take care of themselves when they are healing. They are:

1. Taking care of your essence
2. Taking care of your body and beauty
3. Taking care of your feelings
4. Taking care of your spiritual self
5. Taking care of your social self

Let's take a look at how to take care of your body and beauty. This means taking care of your physical self. Your body deserves to be treated with love, respect, and gentleness, and it deserves to be kept healthy, fit, and beautiful. To maintain health, your body requires good food, exercise, and rest.

Addressing Immediate Concerns

You already know that you poison your body when you drink too much alcohol, smoke too many cigarettes, do too many drugs, or eat unhealthful foods. If substances or overindulgence are a problem for you, think about how you might better take care of yourself. Think about taking care of your body as a way of showing yourself some tenderness and the respect you deserve. As you learn to treat your own body with tenderness and respect, you will attract those who also treat their bodies with tenderness and respect and who can treat you that way. Choosing to be around people who bring a positive influence to your life is one way to help yourself out of situations with drugs and alcohol.

Attracting the Good

During the survival stage some women try to hide or become invisible so as not to attract attention. This is understandable, since the type of attention you have been used to getting has not been positive. Some women who have been violated gain weight in an attempt to make themselves less attractive to men, or in an attempt to fill an emotional void with food, or rebel against limits.

As you heal and reclaim who you are, your natural inner and outer beauty will shine. Embrace the concept that no one can put limits on you, except you. With this knowledge, you can make new decisions about your body and what your body means. This awareness can allow you to attract the attention you desire. You'll need to determine your own sense of what your body needs and what beauty means to you. This is a good time to practice reconnecting with your personal preferences and goals as you define them, and to practice using power language, so you can ask for what you need. Here are some common ways that women can take care of their bodies and beauty:

- Fix their hair
- Wear makeup
- Eat healthy foods
- Cut out refined sugar and fast foods
- Meditate
- Take vitamins
- Engage in activities that are restorative
- Take a dance class

ACTIVITY: *Take a Bath*

Baths aren't just for little kids! Put in bubbles if you have them and baking soda if you don't. Either way, you will feel like a million bucks. Grab a magazine before you close the bathroom door. Or light some candles and turn off the lights. As you soak, feel the warm water on your skin and think pleasant thoughts. Let your mind wander and conjure before your eyes a life of love, happiness, and joy. Use this prompt to get you started: "I love myself. I am beautiful. I enjoy taking care of my body by . . ."

ACTIVITY: *Beautiful Body Self-Talk*

Body image is a common source of negative self-talk for all types of women. Just like with any negative thoughts, you need to stop negative body-image thoughts as soon as they arise. Use your mental stop sign to redirect those thoughts into positive ones. Don't forget to think of an image to help you think of the positive.

Negative Voice	STOP	Positive Voice
You're so ugly	STOP. Ask yourself: Whose voice is that? Do you want that person and their voice in your head anymore? You get to decide.	Speak Your Truth: I am not ugly. I have a great smile and a beautiful nose! (Image: I see my smile and the way people respond to me when I use it!) And offer a replacement: I am beautiful!!!

Negative Voice	STOP	Positive Voice

A Time to Reflect

Reflection on the steps we take toward Thriving is important. By frequently taking stock of the changes you are making, you can be mindful of the changes that intentionally come from you and are becoming a part of you. You call the shots for this leg of your life journey. Though you want to focus on moving forward, stopping to look at the progress you've made is a great way to celebrate your successes and identify your next steps.

Reflecting on the changes you have made so far is an important step in recognizing those thoughts and beliefs that are new to you. It also helps as a benchmark on your journey.

ACTIVITY: *Reflecting*

Think back on the activities you completed in this unit to discover which has been the most helpful for you. Can you put into words why it was helpful? Recognizing what helped you make important changes means that you can focus on that piece to help you make future changes. You might also reflect on the transformation you have experienced in your life right now and celebrate it.

What has changed for you?

_____

_____

_____

What new picture or image of yourself is emerging?

_____

_____

_____

How have your thoughts changed?

_____

_____

_____

What has changed in your living, work, or family environment? For example, did you get a job? Do you have a new
place to live?

_____

_____

_____

What activities do you want to repeat and why?

_____

_____

_____

Which activity taught you the most about yourself?

_____

_____

_____

How might you celebrate or mark the changes you've made
so far?

_____

_____

_____

Reclaim Your Right to Your Future

"We are shaped by our thoughts; we become what we think. When the mind is pure, joy follows like a shadow that never leaves."

—Buddha

In this unit, you will:

- Expand on joy as a way to create change
- Continue to author change in your life
- Develop goals to help you get there
- Take care of your feelings

Joy!!

In Unit 3, we talked about the idea that you can't sell from an empty cart. In other words, it is hard to summon the energy necessary to heal when you feel depleted, stressed, hopeless, and fearful. Instead, we suggested that changes are made when we feel supported, happy, well cared for, and confident. In Unit 3, we also talked about how using your imagination can go a long way to filling up an empty cart. In this unit, we will talk about the importance of joy. It is another important part of what goes into your cart.

How Language Impacts Your Body

Read the following series of words out loud. As you say them, pay attention to the way you feel inside your body. Pay attention to your muscles, your stomach, your chest, the weight on your shoulders, the way your face feels. Ready? Go ahead.

> **Open Up!**
>
> **Relax!**
>
> **Laugh!**
>
> **Let Go!**
>
> **Relief!**
>
> **Happy!**
>
> **Expand!**
>
> **Joy!**

What did it feel like to say those words?

Violation teaches women to tense up, hunker down, and constrict. Unfortunately, we get so used to doing this that we lose track of the way it feels and how it shapes our outlook on the world around us. So, for comparison purposes, try saying an opposite set of words. Again, pay attention to the way your body feels when you read these words. Pay special attention to your muscles, your stomach, your chest, the weight on your shoulders, the way your face feels.

> **Cry**
> **Worry**
> **Fret**
> **Sad**
> **Brace**
> **Hunker Down**
> **Scared**
> **Tighten**
> **Hopeless**

Did you notice a difference in the way your body felt as you said those words? We hope so—but not because we want you to feel bad. Quite the opposite! We want you to feel great. By noticing how you feel when you focus on the negative, you can learn to recognize those feelings as they creep into your body and your vocabulary and stop them. This will take practice and involves silencing those negative messages you hear inside your head and stopping the negative feelings that come with them.

Noticing the way words and feelings are connected to your body is an important step along the way to making conscious choices about how you want to feel. As you assemble more and more of the foundation of your future, your ability to stay in control of the energy you create and language you use is important.

Your Choices Make You

Just as you make choices about other aspects of your life, you can also make choices about how you feel. If you don't want to live feeling scared and sad and hopeless, you don't have to. In fact, you deserve better than that. You have already made huge changes to create a new direction in your life and write new, positive chapters.

Words and thoughts are connected to the way we act on the world around us. Your words and thoughts shape the way you act, shape the way the world responds to you, and therefore help shape your future. One way to build good thoughts about you and the world around you is to find the positive in everything—then pass it on!

Pay It Forward!

One of the most surprising sources of power and joy you have is to pay your good fortune forward, both verbally and spiritually. Even as you are in the process of healing, when it can be difficult to see the joy you have, it's important to find it and share it. When you can recognize and acknowledge joy in your life, you increase your own joy by helping other women do the same thing. The more you do this, the better you'll be able to see a bright future that is filled with the same joy and happiness that you are giving to others. After all, the energy you share with the universe is the same energy you'll have in your own life.

How to Spread Joy

Sharing joy is simple and easy to do. In the course of your day, reach out and help someone see joy. Start by paying a compliment. It is free, it is easy, and it pays your own gratitude forward. For example, when Danielle goes to the grocery store and the clerks are working hard to ring up the groceries and bag them, she notices something about them—fingernails, hairstyle, glasses, smile, lipstick, speed, and pays a compliment: "Your fingernails look great today!" or "What a perfect shade of lipstick." Or "Thank you so much for your help," or "Wow, your hair looks super today."

Why is complimenting someone else an important part of finding your own joy? When you compliment someone, you share your joy with someone else. When you are able to recognize and acknowledge joy, it just feels natural to share it with others. Laughing at a joke is a wonderful experience. But having someone to share a joke with is actually even better because two of you can connect and share a sense of meaning. Your joy is actually doubled. When you share your joy, you get two gifts: You get to feel your own joy and you have the plea-sure of sharing it with someone else and seeing theirs.

When you share your joy with others, you begin to see that joy is not only abundant—it is actually limitless. So shar-ing it doesn't decrease what you have—it actually increases or multiplies it! By paying joy and happiness forward it helps surround you with good feelings and positive energy, which will help you build your ideal future.

Joy Brings Community

Sharing your joy also reduces your sense of isolation or aloneness, which can be prevalent as you heal from a violating relationship. We often walk through our days believing we are alone or somehow on our own. The experience of being violated makes you feel so different from others that you start believing you *are* different. Feeling different from others increases your isolation. You begin to think you are the only one who has ever gone through this. Finding connections with others from this perspective can be difficult. But when you share joy, the wonderful abundant universe is connecting you with others. Complimenting someone is a way to reach out to someone else in a positive and rewarding way and connect with others. We are, after all, all humans on a similar journey.

Complimenting someone also reminds you to look for what is right rather than what is wrong. When you feel insecure or inadequate, you often look for the negative in others. You may even subconsciously think that if you can find something wrong with other people, it means what's wrong with you or your life isn't so bad. "Survivor thinking" suggests that if you can bring someone else down, then you can hold yourself up. But when you feel really happy inside and you look for what is right, it helps you shift your thinking from disaster- and problem-centered thinking to positive- and what-is-right-oriented thinking. And, since the tenor of your thoughts helps dictate the tenor of your life and future, you want to encourage the positive! By complimenting others, you give yourself permission to see what is right about you and what is right about the world around you.

Work to Find the Joy

At times, you might find it difficult to pay a compliment to someone you don't like very much. But keep this in mind: We don't always like everything about some people. But people are multidimensional. When you focus on the negative, on the bad qualities in people, you make their good qualities seem much smaller. You only see one dimension as you actually enlarge the negative. Thus, you create a negative spiral. Instead, find the positive.

For example, Danielle worked with a group of women in transitional housing. They did not like the caseworker who ran the housing facility. They said she was manipulative and mean. That was all they ever said about her. But this caseworker was a complicated person. Yes, she may have been manipulative and mean—but she was a host of other things, too. When Danielle pushed the women to list some of her other qualities, they came up with words like dedicated, hardworking, caring, concerned, passionate, and tries hard. By focusing on her positive characteristics, they made them larger in their minds and they acted differently toward her. Guess how she responded? She began to act differently toward the women in return. The women created a positive spiral, and effectively changed their future! Instead of enduring a difficult relationship with this woman, they made their lives and hers better by focusing on what was positive and good.

There will be days when this is easier than others, but it is a skill that you can practice. Let's give it a try now.

ACTIVITY: *Compliments for Everyone!*

Here is another activity that asks you to compliment someone as a way of reaching out and connecting with others. Whether you are working by yourself or in a group of other women, it is time to give some compliments and let someone know you are grateful for what she brings to your life. Go ahead, get started!

1. If you are working by yourself, make a list of folks you would like to compliment. Practice in private and then give it a try in real life. Start by noticing what is really right or good or impressive about someone. Even if you may not like everything about the person, you can at least find something good about them. Give it a try.

2. Now, compliment yourself. Take those three great things that you noticed about yourself in the previous exercise and turn them into a compliment. For example, if you said you cook well, add some appreciation and gratitude, and say something like: "Wow! My cooking is wonderful. I am so grateful for this skill!"

   Now you try:
   Taking stock: What was the result of these compliments? Did you laugh? Did people smile? Did you feel energy change? Did you feel the positive grow?

   _____

   _____

   _____

   _____

   _____

_____

_____

_____

_____

_____

_____

_____

_____

_____

_____

_____

ACTIVITY: _I See It!!_

This activity is contagious and often creates tons of good feelings. Get ready for some smiles. Recognizing the positive isn't always easy. Think back to earlier exercises you've done and write down three things that are awesome about you.

1. _____
2. _____
3. _____

Now take inventory of those with whom you live or some coworkers. List some positives about them.

1. _____
2. _____
3. _____

And now think about this day. What went right about it?

1. _____
2. _____
3. _____

Take a look at this list. What makes you feel grateful? Take a moment to really feel this gratitude. Where in your body do you feel it? What does it feel like? Now, in your journal, write a statement or two about your gratitude. After doing this activity, what are you grateful for?

ACTIVITY: *Accepting Compliments*

Now there is the issue of accepting compliments to consider. Now that you've given out all sorts of wonderful compliments to other people, pay attention to how you respond when someone compliments you. Do you even hear the compliment? Is your first reaction to minimize whatever it is you are being complimented for? Karen found she had to work on this. When she is complimented, her first response is to shake her head, roll her eyes, and say "Oh, yeah." She has to remind herself to stop, listen, and say "Thank you."

Here are some additional tips: Remind yourself not to deflect the compliment. It is yours. Claim it. Don't offer excuses why whatever is being complimented isn't really as good as the person thinks it is. This is your moment, so take it. Feel good about being recognized. Finally, you can be as embarrassed as you want, but your response needs to be clear, confident, and appreciative.

The next time you are complimented, stop, listen, stand up tall, and say, "Thank you!" If you are working with a group of women, take the opportunity to practice this skill with them. If you are working by yourself, stand in front of a mirror to practice.

You really do deserve the compliment. And by receiving a compliment you are asked to reflect joy back to someone. The universe operates through this kind of wonderful symmetry!

Take Steps to Reclaim Your Future

Through your ability to dream and maintain and protect positive energy, you can envision a new life for yourself and call it to you. Remember, this power gains strength and magnitude through enactment. The more you practice it, the more good things will come to you. The more you practice thinking and acting positively, the more things in your external world will change to mirror the reality in your head. When you first begin, it will feel like you are writing fiction or dreaming "too big." Keep going. These fictions will become realities. Many practitioners, counselors, leaders, and inspirational speakers have utilized this principle. It is not new, but it is revolutionary!

In order to implement a new future, you need to take things in small steps. In an earlier activity, you listed your values and your interests. You also wrote a letter to yourself about your ideal life in the future. Now is the time to think about how you can integrate those values, interests, and visions of perfection into a plan for your future.

This next activity helps you bring into focus those things that you truly desire in your life. It always helps to start with a list. You can add to it, you can delete an item if your interests change, and by writing it down, you create it in the external world where it can begin to take shape and form.

ACTIVITY: *I Desire!*

Make a list of all the things you most desire in your life right now. It might be a job, a home, a relationship, or a career.

1. _____
2. _____
3. _____

Circle the thing that is the most important to you at this time.

Now, can you flesh it out? In other words, can you write down some of the specifics about that one thing? For example, if it is a place to live, can you describe it? Where will it be located? What kind of floors might it have? Does it have a yard? Can you write down its major characteristics or features? Be as specific as you can.

_____
_____
_____
_____

How will you feel once you have this in your life? Write down your feelings.

_____

_____

_____

_____

What would happen if you acted that way now? What would change in your life? What would people see when they looked at you? Here is why we ask. We tend to think, *If I get this, then I will be happy.* But you already know that your thoughts shape your reality, and waiting for that day to come postpones joy and puts you in the passive position of just waiting. If you were happy, grateful, and relieved now, you would act grateful, happy, and relieved. Get a good mental picture of that joyful state where what you desire has come to pass. Feel those feelings. Know that it can and will happen.

Stay in Touch with Your Courage

Every book you have ever read or enjoyed began as a blank piece of paper. Many writers would say that's a very scary thing to look at! In fact, any author will tell you that it takes courage to look at a blank page and believe you can create a whole new world on it. The same is true for the authorship involved in creating your new life. It takes courage to start down a new path, courage to believe new things, courage to have faith that you can actually reach your goals. As you think about the life changes you have made up to this point, think about what courage you have shown to face your fears. This courage is an important part of authorship and reclaiming your identity, life path, and future.

You also must stare down your fears. A writer named Ambrose Redmoon said, "Courage is not the absence of fear, but rather the judgment that something else is more important than fear." In this case, building your new life is more important than your fears. It's okay to acknowledge your doubts and uncertainties as a natural part of your healing process, but you must also push beyond them.

As you author a new life for yourself, you are called to create and called to let your unique light and power shine in the world. While living in a violating relationship you probably discovered very quickly that in order to survive you had to hide that light, cover up your brilliance, pretend you were not competent. Not anymore. Your future depends on your ability to let your wonderful, joyful, creative self come out.

ACTIVITY: *Celebrate Your Successes Thus Far*

It's a great idea to step back every once in a while and acknowledge the progress you've made. In this activity, list the important life changes you have made or steps you have taken in spite of your fears.

_____

_____

_____

Ask Your Inner Child for Help

Authoring a new future for yourself is necessarily creative work. Let's face it, when you are trying to create a whole new life based on a whole new way of thinking about yourself and the world, you are going to have to be creative!

For some women, getting in touch with your inner creative child helps move the process along. When we are children, we create without worrying about whether or not what we create is "right" or whether it looks like the thing we are imagining. We simply create and often, if we are lucky, lose ourselves to the process. The minute we worry about whether or not it is good enough or done right, we change the product. In fact, we infuse the product with worry and anxiety and doubt. This is something that is learned and can be unlearned. One trick of authorship is to get in touch with that childlike creativity, that whimsy, and simply begin.

Make a Date with Silliness

Your inner child is an important treasure. How has she been a guide for you in your life changes thus far? How might she be a guide for you in the future?

In order to get in touch with her, take a moment to think about those childlike qualities you have hung on to that may need to take front and center for a while. Is it drawing? Is it being silly? Is it laughing at stupid jokes? Is it dressing up with your kids? Whatever it is, take time to be silly and child-like now. Once you have done it, write it down.

- My inner child and I . . .
- My inner child and I . . .

Revisit your inner child whenever you feel like your creativity needs a boost. She can help you refocus on the simple things in life and dream big without censoring yourself.

Reward Yourself!

Growth and change is hard work. It can be joyful work, but it is work nonetheless. It is so important to be kind with and to yourself and to reward yourself in positive, healthy, and helpful ways. You are going through enormous changes as you reclaim your future. Giving yourself a reward is the intentional act of filling up your cart.

Why Reward Yourself?

When money is tight and life is hectic, rewarding yourself easily moves to the back burner. But it is really important to move it to the front because you deserve it.

It is very important to recognize those moments when you have done something wonderful, or monumental, or difficult. As you move your life in a direction that feels right, it is important to step back and acknowledge your successes, no matter how small they seem at the time. Taking stock helps you recognize that indeed you are on the right path and you have made a stride. Think about it like climbing a ladder. At each rung, you must acknowledge that you have gained some altitude! Otherwise, how will you know where you are?

How to Reward Yourself

As you consider what you might do to treat yourself, remember it doesn't have to be expensive or high calorie. It simply must feel intentional and intentionally rewarding. It might also be a little unusual. Is there a free concert in your community? Is there a trip to the library you have been putting off? Now is the time. As you treat yourself let yourself know that this is for all you have accomplished so far.

- My rewards:

_____

_____

_____

_____

_____

_____

_____

_____

Have Patience

Taking a journey as monumental as reclaiming your future takes patience. This is not the same as waiting, however. Patience means that you give yourself time to heal, time to make the changes that healing requires of you. *Waiting* implies that you are passively sitting by while life passes you. *Patience* implies that you're giving yourself the time and space to imagine your future in a thoughtful, healthy way.

Following is an activity that helps you reclaim your future by focusing your attention on your abilities and strengths. Much like the pledge of allegiance we used to say as schoolchildren, this activity is a way of professing your strength.

A mantra is a word or a phrase used in some religions that help people make transformation. We've written a Brilliance mantra for you to recite as a reminder of the power you have and the future you're creating. You might want to do the Belly Breathing Basics activity explained in Unit 3 before reading this aloud. That way, you're relaxed and centered and able to focus on it. But you certainly don't have to. Once you have said this mantra out loud a few times, find a gesture to go with it. This will become your Brilliance gesture. It might be wiggling your fingers in a "sparkle" gesture. Or it might be the snap of your fingers. Just a little something to get your body to work with your mouth and brain.

Brilliance Mantra

I will let the world see my Brilliance, know my power, feel my joy.

I will shine my light for all to see.

I will never again be ashamed of being smart, or knowledgeable, or funny or savvy, or competent.

I am all of these things and I claim them with pride. I am grateful for my gifts and I will use them for the benefit of myself, my family, and the world.

These gifts are mine and I will never hide them or pretend they were not given to me. These gifts are mine and I claim them and make space for them in my life. These gifts are mine and I build my life in and through them.

I am power and joy and competence and Brilliance.

I shine.

If you're feeling artsy, grab those magazines or pens and paints. Make a collage or beautiful work of art to help you illustrate this mantra. The more creative you are—the better. For it is in your creative activities that you release your innate creative abilities. As you create the illustration for your Brilliance mantra, see if you can include the ideas we learned above: courage, let your inner playfulness emerge, treat yourself, be patient with yourself, and remember that as the author of your own life, you are creative and creating!

ACTIVITY: *Inner Child Meditation*

We have talked several times in this workbook about your inner child. It is an important concept because it captures the idea that you already have inside you the knowledge, power, wisdom, and creativity you need in order to change your life for the better. We want to emphasize this inner wisdom. It belongs to you. It *is* you. Violation can separate you from that knowledge and can teach you to stop listening to your own inner wisdom. Therefore, getting in touch with that aspect of yourself offers you a way to recenter your life on positive, playful, and joyful truths and to access important strengths and insights you can use to build your future.

This meditation comes from *A Gentle Path through the Twelve Steps* (Hazelden: Center City, Minnesota) and is used with permission of the author, Patrick Carnes. We asked to include it in its entirety because as we were traversing our own healing journey, we found it quite helpful. The author of this meditation suggests that through the use of metaphors we can tap the inner playful child and access powerful healing images.

See how it is for you. See what you can learn about yourself. Find a nice comfortable position.

If you are feeling anything emotionally distressing, picture yourself putting it in a box and setting it aside until the meditation is over. [pause]

Get in touch with your own bodily rhythms, your breathing, your heart rate. With each breath you take, each beat of your heart, you are participating in the larger rhythms of the universe. Each of those beats, each of those rhythms, has a sacredness to it because it is part of the forces of the universe. [pause]

Imagine that you are lying in a meadow on a summer day. You can feel the sun on your body. You feel very, very peaceful. You can hear the birds singing, smell the flowers and the grasses of the field. [pause]

You feel beckoned, as if you are being asked to go somewhere. You hear a voice calling you. You gently sit up. You look around. At the end of the meadow is a road. You know that road is where you need to go. You get up and walk to the road at the edge of the meadow. You walk down the road. As you walk, you come around the corner to a lake where there is a beach. There is a child playing in the sand on the beach. [pause]

As you approach, you see something familiar about that child. You leave the road. As you come close, you see that the child is you at the age of five. This is what you looked like. This is who you were at the age of five. You get down on your knees and look at the child at the child's level, and you ask the child how the child is doing.

What does the child say to you? [pause]

Walk with the child. Invite the child to come along with you on your journey. Reach out and offer the child your hand. Ask the child to join you. The two of you leave the beach and go on down the road. [pause]

As you walk down the road, you come to some large hills at the base of a mountain. Up on one of the hills is a large, sanctuary-like building. You and the child approach the building. There is a long flight of stairs; a man and a woman walk out. They are so peaceful looking. They say, "Come, we have been waiting for you." You and the child walk up the stairs, and the man and woman each take your hands and say, "We're so glad you are here."

Now they invite you in. They say, "We want to take you to what we call the room of visions." They guide you into a room with multicolored glass in the ceiling and skylights. There is no furniture, but a soft, spongy floor and four walls. [pause]

Your guides ask you to sit down. They explain to you that the room of visions is a way to have windows into your life.

The woman guide turns to your child and asks, "What is hurting you?" [pause] "How do you hurt right now?"

What does your child say to the woman right now? [pause]

The man turns to you and asks, "What is troubling you?" [pause]

What do you say to the man? [pause]

Then the woman explains, "We brought you here because we know you are troubled and we believe that there are things you already know that can help. Each wall to this room contains a vision. Two of the walls have visions of your future. Let's look at the first one."

The wall dissolves and there is an image of your future. You are watching you in your own future. What is this image about? [pause] What is happening in your future? [pause] What do you see? [pause] How do you react to this vision of the future? [pause] Look at your child. How is your child reacting to the vision from the future? [pause] The man says to you, "Now remember, you can choose whether you want this in your future. Make a decision."

Look at your child. Is the child comfortable? [pause] Look at your future. Do you want this as part of your future? [pause] Make your decision and, as you decide, watch as the wall goes blank.

The guides then point to another wall. It dissolves and another vision comes out of your future. What is happening in this vision? [pause] What are you doing? [pause] Who are you with? [pause] How does it look like you are feeling in this future? [pause] How do you feel watching it? How does your child feel? [pause] Look at your child. How is your child reacting to it? [pause]

The woman says to you, "Now again you can make a decision. Is this what you want?" [pause] "Is this what you want in your future?" [pause] "Choose." As you make your decision, the wall becomes opaque again. [pause]

The man says, "Behind the third wall are gifts. The child is to go first." The wall dissolves and there is a gift waiting for the child. What is the gift? [pause] "This is a spiritual gift," the man says. "Have your child go and get the gift and then come back and sit down on the soft, warm floor."

As you look up, your other guide says, "There is a gift in there for you, a spiritual gift. Let it be a symbol for you." What is the gift? [pause] What does it look like? [pause] What characteristics does it have? [pause] Get up and walk over to the gift. Pick it up and bring it back.

Behind the fourth wall, your guide says, "Picture an animal that you think is like you. An animal that can have a special significance." Your child goes first. What animal appears for your child? [pause] Your guide asks, "How are you like this animal?" [pause] "In what ways are you like this animal?" [pause]

Now it is your turn. What animal fits for you? [pause] The wall dissolves and you can picture that animal. What is it like? [pause] How are you like that animal? [pause] What characteristics does it have that are like you? [pause]

Your guide says, "Let these animals serve as symbols for you of what you are about. Learn about them. Study them. They will teach you what you need to know."

You and your guides rise and you walk out of the building, into a garden, and down the stairs. You sit down next to your child. Spend a little time now, talking to that child. What do the Healers say to that child? [pause] What did you learn? [pause] How can you use the gifts? [pause] What about the future? Talk to the child. [pause]

As you finish your conversation, take the child's hand and walk back to the beach.

Promise your child that you will let your child play, but that you will leave now. Whenever that child needs you, you will be back. Promise that the Healer within you will always be there for the child. [pause]

As you walk about, back towards the meadow, you are aware that something has shifted. Something will never be the same. You feel steadier. You trust yourself. You are more peaceful. Sturdier. As you lay down in the meadow, you can feel the presence of the moment, how you blend into the earth, embracing it. You decide to rest and you go to sleep.

When you are ready to finish the fantasy, awake and arise slowly and peacefully. Hold on to the feelings of your imagery.

- What images came to you during this meditation?

_____

_____

_____

_____

- What gifts did you receive? Why do you think you received them?

_____

_____

_____

_____

_____

- What animals are your special animals?

_____

_____

_____

_____

_____

- What knowledge or insight will you take from this meditation into your waking life that can help you right now?

_____

_____

_____

_____

_____

A Mission Statement for Your Future

Many businesses or organizations create a mission statement for themselves. A mission statement helps an organization define who they are and helps them know where they are going.

You can use this same philosophy to make your own personal mission statement. It can be a guide that helps you clarify your purpose, especially since that purpose may have changed as you have gone through the healing process, as well as a declaration of your future direction.

The following activity can easily be adapted to include other family members if you want to develop a family mission statement! The following exercise gives some prompts to get you thinking about what's important to you, but the list is not exhaustive. You may find that some of the questions apply to you, while you wish to disregard others. Only use those that feel right to you!

ACTIVITY: *Write Your Own Mission Statement*

List three strengths you have that are very important to you and that will help you create the life you want to have. For example: hard work, honesty, dedication, courage.

1. _____

2. _____

3. _____

Next, finish these sentences.

I am at my best when . . .

_____

_____

The activity I enjoy the most is . . .

_____

_____

In my life I want to make sure I spend lots of time . . .

_____

_____

If I had no other responsibilities one day (week, month), I would . . .

_____

_____

If my home could be filled with one emotion, it would be . . .

_____

_____

List three gifts or strengths you would like others to use when describing you:

_____

_____

She is _____ and _____
and _____

I am very unique in this way . . .

_____

_____

Think for a minute about the ideal life you imagined in Unit 3. Answer these questions about your future:

Financially, I am . . .

_____

_____

I am in a relationship with someone who I . . .

_____

_____

Spiritually, I . . .

_____

_____

Next, review the answers you have given, and think about them as a whole picture rather than parts to a picture. Are there some patterns? Do some things come up over and over? For example, if you notice that loving family relationships are important, you may choose to include the words family and love in your mission statement. You may want to follow this general outline or you may want to use your creativity to shape something completely different. This can get you started creating your own mission statement.

I [your name], believe that my purpose is to [whatever you find most important]. I will accomplish this through [this is a good place for those characteristics]. What comes next in your

---

How Do I Get There from Here?

This next part of reclaiming your future is to figure out how to get from where you are now to where you want to be. In several activities in the book, you have fleshed out your ideal place to live or a job that would be perfect for you or a great relationship. In Unit 3, you described in a letter your perfect life. Now it is time to create a map that will help you navigate your way there.

If you have ever taken a long trip, you know that it often starts by looking at a map and seeing where you want to go. In some cases, you might trace your route from your destination back to your starting point. This is what we are going to do with your goals.

Try Starting at the End

Starting at the end may seem counterintuitive, but it can actually be quite effective in helping you define your goals. For example, Danielle is the director of a large program at her university that often needs to be revised and updated. These changes can get complicated, as they involve a lot of people and a lot of details. It helps her to think about what the program should look like when it is finished (visualizing the end product). With that picture in mind, she traces her way back to where the program is at the present. In the next activity, you get a chance to try this type of backward thinking!

The Benefits of Starting at the End

A lot of goal-setting experts agree that when you start from the present and look to the future and try to set goals, they can quickly become overwhelming. By the time you have listed the goal and tried to figure out the next step, it is easy to feel defeated. So, this time, try setting goals in reverse. This makes sense since we have done so much thinking about the future and what a perfect future might look like. This is what we want you to do in the following activity.

Some women find it helpful to actually make a map. Others find it helpful to make a calendar. We'll give you directions for both ways. There is no right or wrong way to set goals for yourself. Some women really enjoy this activity and others prefer to make it up as they go along. Do whatever works best for you.

You can make your map as detailed as you want it to be. In our experience, the more detailed the better. Putting in as many details as you can helps you see where you are heading more clearly. You can refer to this map as your guide as often as you need to. Also, you can use it to visualize the future, and to create a positive intention about your future.

To get started, take a large piece of paper. On the right-hand side of the paper, write FINISH. Underneath it, write down one very important goal you want to achieve. It can be a great place to live or a perfect job or a wonderful relationship. Choose one thing to focus on for now (you can make as many of these maps as you wish!).

On the very left-hand side of the paper, write START. Underneath it, write down where you are in relation to this goal. (Use pencil so you can erase and reorder as you need to.) It might be words like "no job," or "a temporary living arrangement," or "with no partner."

Now it's time to make your map. Starting at the FINISH line, work your way steadily back toward the START line by writing down milestones you will achieve on your way to your goal.

Remember, you are thinking of your journey backward. Starting at the finish line means you will want to ask yourself, *What milestones do I need to accomplish?* So if your FINISH goal is to own your own wonderful home, ask yourself, what did you do right before you turned the key in the lock and crossed the threshold of your very own home? You probably signed papers at the bank. What did you do before that? You probably secured a bank loan. And before that? Keep working your way toward the START line.

After you have the major milestones completed, go back and fill in the gaps. This is also a good time to flesh out the details. If one of your stops along the way to a new home was to get a great job, you might want to flesh this out by writing underneath "get a job" what this might look like. It might look like this: "Get a great job at the library shelving books and organizing files." Or "Get a great job helping women who are fleeing domestic violence." (Or, you could set up a separate map entirely for that goal.) If the step before that is to go back to school, be specific. Where will you go to school? What will you major in? How might you find out about financial aid? This is what we mean when we say, filling in the gaps.

ACTIVITY: *Reflecting on Your Map*

Take a look at your goal and the road to it. Did anything surprise you about this path?

_____

_____

How does it feel to see the road laid out in this way? Does it seem achievable?

_____

_____

Do you have a sense of where you will start?

_____

_____

Are there any places on the road you have laid out that might need to be refined?

_____

_____

Do you need to add some steps or change some steps? You might want to do that now.

_____

_____

ACTIVITY: *Calendar of Goals*

Here is another way to approach goal setting. Create a twelve-month calendar that outlines a goal you want to accomplish. You might try assembling twelve pieces of paper, one for each month. You can also get an actual calendar and make it your own by personalizing it.

To start, pick your goal and write it in the last month of your calendar. Now work your way backward toward the month you are currently in. On each month, write the steps you will take that month to achieve your goal. Again, we have found that it helps to use as much detail as you can. You might consider assigning a purpose to a month to make sure you highlight certain things. For example, June might be "find a new place to live month" or "find out about going back to school month." March might be "apply for my new job month."

As you do this activity, think about the obstacles that pop into your mind. How can you turn those obstacles into other goals? For example, if your goal is to find a great job in social work, but you lack the education needed (obstacle), how might that obstacle become a goal? Is it time to head back to school? If that is the case, then where will you put that on your calendar?

_____

_____

_____

_____

_____

_____

Release Positive Energy

Now that you see the path before you, whether in road map or calendar form, it is important to turn the vision into positive energy. Think about your end goal and create a positive state ment to help you. It might be something like: *I have the job of my dreams. The job of my dreams will come to me.*

When making your positive energy statement, stay away from language that will attract deficiency or lacking like, "want," "need," or "don't have," and replace it with language that attracts abundance, such as *I will have, I will attract, I have.*

As you work to create a new and perfect or ideal future for yourself, it is a good thing to remember that you aren't the first one to do this. George Eliot, a writer who lived more than 100 years ago, said, "It is never too late to be who you might have been." So as you continue to reclaim and create a life for yourself, know that you stand in a proud tradition of people who have done just what you are doing.

The Importance of Self-Care: Taking Care of Your Feelings

In Unit 3, we introduced the idea that there are five ways women take care of themselves when they are healing. They are:

1. Taking care of your essence
2. Taking care of your body and beauty
3. Taking care of your feelings
4. Taking care of your spiritual self
5. Taking care of your social self

In this unit, we focus on taking care of your feelings. Taking care of your feelings requires that you take time out to identify, reflect upon, understand, interpret, trust, and accept your feelings. This occurs at two levels.

1. One level involves understanding our emotional reactions to things.
2. The second level involves understanding how our emotions, responses, and choices form life patterns.

Writing in a journal is an excellent way to reflect on your feelings and to connect feelings to your responses. It is also a way of identifying some of the underlying issues that shape your responses.

Healthy Journaling Techniques
Some women tell us that they have kept feeling journals for years yet don't feel any better for having done so. When

we ask what they write in their journals, they tell us that their journals are full of angst, pain, sadness, and despair. We would never tell you *not* to keep a journal for your most private thoughts and feelings, but one filled with sadness will probably not help you achieve happiness. At a certain point, it is time to create something different in your life with the help of a different kind of journal or a different kind of attention to your feelings.

Feeling good takes practice and coming from the survival stage, you may be out of practice. Learn to recognize what makes you feel good and repeat it. Here are some ways to do that:

- Consider starting a new journal of your triumphs. Feel free to record the bumps you hit along the way. But keep your eyes on the ideal future you're building.
- Find a regular time to write. For some of us it is in the morning, before the kids are up, when we are having morning coffee. We reflect on the activities of the day before and write down our hopes for the coming day. Others write at the end of the day. Either way, trying to find a regular quiet time will help you get in the groove of journaling.
- Start by thinking and writing about an accomplishment, however trivial it may seem, that you achieved during the day. Write down what was difficult and how you felt about it. Make sure to "link" the accomplishment with a future goal you have.

Managing Negative Feelings

It is important to acknowledge your negative feelings without dwelling on them or being consumed by them. If something makes you feel bad or sad, then avoid it, whether it is a movie, a book, a person, an activity, a topic of conversation, or anything else that gives you that sinking, icky, frightened feeling. You do not have to participate in things that make you feel bad. You are in control of yourself and the world around you. For example:

- You do not have to watch the movie you rented; if it makes you feel uncomfortable, turn it off.
- If that painting on your wall makes you sad, donate it to a thrift shop and hang up a picture that makes you feel good.
- Be open to humor; science has shown it is healing to laugh. Feeling embarrassed? Instead of hanging your head, throw it back and let loose some wild laughter. If that makes you feel good, do it the next time, too.

Often, feelings of anger and resentment can be traced back to fear and shame; fear of being unworthy or not good enough and the shame of being discovered. Fear and shame act as barriers that prevent you from accepting the gifts and happiness you are entitled to—because you do not feel that you deserve them. This creates a negative spiral. Our goal in thriving is to create a positive spiral. As you become more confident and certain in your healing, you know that you do deserve to be happy and to receive wonderful things in your future.

"Feeling" Glasses
Try to imagine feelings as empty glasses lined up in front of you at the start of each day. Some glasses are marked "bitterness," "worry," "anger," and "sadness." Others are marked "happiness," "calm," "joy," "laughter," "love," and "gratitude."

You can pour as much or as little in them as you wish all day long. At the end of the day, you get to keep whatever glasses you have filled and drink them down. Which glass would you like to drink from today? Choose which glass to fill up—meaning, choose which feelings to invest your time and energy in.

Remember, focusing your attention on something makes it grow, so be sure you are focusing on the good feelings. This is not to say you should avoid challenges or difficult tasks; daring to embrace and complete complex or demanding missions can help you feel stronger in the new life you have chosen. Be aware of your emotions and emphasize the actions that create good feelings for you.

Managing Feelings of Failure

And failures? Oh yes. Expect them! Learn from them and keep moving forward. Failures are simply events. They have nothing to do with defining who you are. Just in case you think that every person in the world succeeded at everything they did the first time they did it—uh—think again! We anticipate wonderful things for and from you. And some of those wonderful things might be delivered in a package that asks you to try again.

ACTIVITY: *My Joyous Journal!*

It is time to start that journal we mentioned. Your first task is to name your journal. And it should be a name that reflects your new stage of life. Here are some suggestions: "My Journal of Hope," "New Beginnings," "Fresh Start," "The Diary of a Thriver."

Begin this way, "Dear (your name), I love you. This is what I want you to know today. . . .

Make sure you date each entry you write! Take the time as often as you can to write to yourself using the prompt.

ACTIVITY: *Rediscover Your Inner Child's Feelings*

This activity can be done in a number of ways. You decide what works best for you. Go through your old photos. Select four or five pictures of you as a child engaged in play. Perhaps you were at the beach, on a swing, or blowing out the candles on a birthday cake. If your childhood was painful, pick pictures of your children in these moments. If you no longer have pictures of you as a child, flip through some magazines of kids having fun. Stop at one that really speaks to you.

Really look at the pictures. Remember where you were, what time of year it was, and what the weather was like. Recall the activity, but more important, remember the feelings and sensations. If you are looking at a magazine picture, imagine what the sensations are for the child in the picture.

Feelings are emotions, sensations are physical experiences and responses. Push yourself to identify five wonderful and joy-filled feelings and sensations drawn from the pictures.

1. _____

2. _____

3. _____

4. _____

5. _____

Now, think of a magnifying glass. Take a few moments to really conjure up a magnifying glass; perhaps remember a time when you played with one as a child. Imagine holding the magnifying glass over the picture and magnifying the feelings and sensations. Magnify the feelings ten times, a hundred times! Imagine that you are having those feelings and sensations now. Get up and start moving. Sing, dance, or laugh out loud. Don't be shy. No one is going to judge!

It may seem silly and that's fine! Remember—your inner child might like a little silly now and again. By getting up and moving around in a silly, celebratory way, you reconnect feelings and sensations to that picture. From now on, carry that picture with you. Whenever you feel stuck, pull out the picture and your imaginary magnifying glass. Recall those feelings and sensations and then if you are able to, get up and dance!

ACTIVITY: *Green, Yellow, Red*

Here is an activity we have used in our healing groups to help women pay attention to the patterns in their own lives and the feelings that can accompany them. We use this activity with permission from the author, Melissa Bradley, who runs the Omnibus Center (*www.omnibuswellness.org*). While we are busy putting one foot in front of the other and starting to create a new life for ourselves, we can find ourselves in a bit of chaos. But Karen and Danielle have both discovered that there are actually predictable patterns in our lives. By recognizing them, we can have some control over them. This activity is designed to help you recognize the patterns that signal the need to alter course.

Your state of mind can be equated to a traffic light. The green zone is when you feel good about life, ready to go! Yellow is in between and could lead to the red zone if not checked. And the red zone is when things are out of control or when you are feeling depressed and blocked.

This exercise is based on the importance of knowing what makes you feel good and what makes you feel bad and how to get yourself or keep yourself feeling good.

If you can identify when you are in a green state and what contributes to that state, you can stay there longer and more often. With the ability to identify when the warnings are sounding you can veer away from yellow back to green and hopefully avoid red altogether.

If you begin to transition from the green zone to the yellow zone, could you get back to green instead of progressing to red? Do you have to transition to red? Can you seek out situations that put you in a green state of mind and avoid situations that put you in a red state of mind? With practice you can make your time in the green zone longer and longer and your time in the red zone short and far between. With knowledge and self-awareness, you can do it. You are in control.

For this exercise, gather magazines, scissors, construction paper, and glue or paste.

1. Divide your construction paper into three parts. The first part will be your green zone, the middle will be your yellow zone part, and the last part will be your red zone.

2. Think about how it feels to be in a green zone, ready to go, ready to take on the world. Now, cut images out of magazines that represent your green zone.
3. Do the same for your yellow zone and your red zone.
4. Paste the images in the appropriate zones on the construction paper.
5. Using your creation, share what the three zones feel like for you and what contributes to each zone. Make a plan to achieve more time in the green zone. What can you do to feel good?

Source: Melissa Bradley, *www.omnibuswellness.org*, 615-377-6002, *Counseling Victims of Sexual Trauma, The Three Stages of Healing*.

Finding Epiphanies

An epiphany is a sudden burst of insight, understanding, or joy. Often people think of epiphanies as life changing, and they can be. But you can also experience "little epiphanies" of joy and happiness that are not life altering, yet remind you of your power and the beauty in the world. In order to fully experience these moments you need to pay attention, recognize when one is presented to you, and be willing to stay in the moment.

For women, little epiphanies often center around those incredibly special, loving moments that happen spontaneously with their children or family. For example, think of a time you were watching or playing with a child and you were able to lose yourself in the moment. There was no place else in the world you wanted to be other than right there at that moment. Perhaps you and the child laughed, or hugged, or just acted silly. When we let ourselves fully experience the feelings of that moment, we are experiencing a little epiphany.

Another time that little epiphanies can happen is when we are outside, experiencing the beauty of nature. Perhaps you are walking by yourself along a beach or along a wooded trail. You feel completely safe and surrounded by the beauty of nature. You feel the sun on your face and the breeze around you. You hear the rustle of the leaves and realize there is no place on earth you would rather be. You experience the epiphany of joy in the moment.

ACTIVITY: *Recognize Epiphanies*

As you go through the next week, be sensitive to these simple moments of living and loving that offer the possibility of a little epiphany. When you start to sense the moment, pay attention. Look around you and notice everything that surrounds you. Let the feeling build in you until it fills you up. Stay there for as long as you can. When you leave the moment, make a conscious effort to take it with you.

Try to have three little epiphanies in the coming week.

What was the moment?

_____

_____

Who were you with (if anyone)?

_____

What was going on around you?

_____

_____

What made the moment special?

_____

_____

How did you feel inside?

_____

_____

How long did you stay in the moment?

_____

_____

Were you able to take the feelings with you throughout the day? The rest of the week? If so, how or what did you do to make it possible?

_____

_____

What if that moment became a symbol of excellence and joy and perfection? Draw or create a self-symbol that reflects that moment using clay, pens, or markers.

A Time to Reflect

Reflection on the steps we take toward Thriving is important. By frequently taking stock of the changes you are making, you can be mindful of the changes that intentionally come from you and are becoming a part of you. You call the shots for this leg of your life journey. Though you want to focus on moving forward, stopping to look at the progress you've made is a great way to celebrate your successes and identify your next steps.

Reflecting on the changes you have made so far is an important step in recognizing those thoughts and beliefs that are new to you. It also helps as a benchmark on your journey.

ACTIVITY: *Reflecting*

Think back on the activities you completed in this unit to discover which has been the most helpful for you. Can you put into words why it was helpful? Recognizing what helped you make important changes means that you can focus on that piece to help you make future changes. You might also reflect on the transformation you have experienced in your life right now and celebrate it.

What has changed for you?

_____

_____

_____

What new picture or image of yourself is emerging?

_____

_____

_____

How have your thoughts changed?

_____

_____

_____

What has changed in your living, work, or family environment? For example, did you get a job? Do you have a new place to live?

_____

_____

_____

What activities do you want to repeat and why?

_____

_____

_____

Which activity taught you the most about yourself?

_____

_____

_____

How might you celebrate or mark the changes you've made so far?

_____

_____

_____

Healing Unit 6

You Are Not Alone: Spirituality, Ritual, and Change

"Re-examine all you have been told. Dismiss what insults your soul."

—WALT WHITMAN

In this unit, you will:

- Explore the powerful and mystical Divine world as a source of strength, encouragement, hope, and guidance
- Connect or reconnect with your intuition and hear the voice of the Divine
- Explore the wonderful and amazing purposes for which you were born

What Is Spirituality?

When we introduce the importance of connecting to a spiritual source in face-to-face groups with women, we often hear women say, "No thanks!" Some women shake their heads no or even physically recoil. Many of these women have had bad experiences with religion. For some, their religion simply didn't support them as they fought desperately to stay alive in an abusive relationship. For others, their religion actively recommended they stay in an abusive relationship no matter the consequences for themselves or their children. When people use religious beliefs as a reason to look the other way or when they misunderstand abuse as something an abuser can stop doing, then religion and religious beliefs become co-conspirators with your batterer and actually help your abuse continue. It is impossible to emerge from the experience with anything other than feelings of anger and disappointment and even revulsion.

Let's take care of some old business first. Are you carrying some heavy religious baggage that you may want to put down? Think for a minute about images of God or angels that you may have. Many of us grew up thinking of God as a wise old man who sat on a throne and judged us. You might have been made to feel unworthy, inferior, imperfect, or inadequate. You may have felt like you never quite did the right thing. You may also have been constantly trying to contain your own impulses. Others may have grown up thinking that only some people—like a priest or a minister—could talk to God and had to interpret God's will or wishes for you. And still others may have grown up thinking that there was a God out there but that God was too hard or too distant or too distracted to hear you. If any of these images and experiences is yours, understand that these are artifacts of religion and do not belong to a sense of personal spirituality.

Organized religion is not the same as spirituality. While there are a lot of religions that will support you as a woman trying to create a new life post-violation, it is important to understand the differences between religion and spirituality and how you can use the latter to help you continue on your journey.

Human beings create religions often based on their interpretations of the divine. But human beings do not create God or the Divine Source. And this is what we want to connect to. This source of all goodness and love and power is what sustains, guides, protects, and feeds us. And quite simply put, it is available to you. This unit offers you one way to connect with that source of infinite abundance.

Getting Started

Sometimes the best way to "ease into" spirituality is to think of a "Divine" being who is simply a perfect friend. If you could imagine a friend, an ideal friend, what would that friend be like? Take a minute to imagine the qualities that friend would possess and list them. Use the following questions as prompts to get you thinking:

- How and in what ways would that friend support you?
- Is that friend always there for you?
- Does that friend always understand you even when you don't understand yourself?

- Is that friend someone who can offer you guidance and support when you most need it?
- Is it someone who is wise and who can help you achieve your dreams and goals?
- Did that friend love you and see the good in you no matter what?

Now, you can begin to think about the Divine in the terms you just defined. This Divine source can really be that amazing an influence in your life—you simply need to ask for it. In that asking, you open yourself up to hear the voice of the Divine.

Preparing Yourself to Be Spiritual

A French Jesuit priest named Tielhard de Chardin is credited with writing, "We are not human beings having a spiritual experience. We are spiritual beings having a human experience." Just as we wrote earlier that you were not born to suffer—you were born to be loved and valued—we must also point out that our human existence is not limited to waking up each morning, going to work or looking for work, paying bills, and putting gas in the car. These are human experiences but they are not the limit of our experience as human beings. And we are not born to simply struggle through everyday routines but to have meaning and connection. Too often in the stress of everyday living, we place all our energy and value on surviving the day, getting the tasks on our to-do list accomplished—and we forget that this is not the sum total of who we are or what we are born to.

We are much more than the routines we established for ourselves. We are spiritual beings. Starting on your spiritual path is the process where you begin to understand that and shift your focus from the routine to the Divine. We are spiritual beings at our core. And we are connected to each other through our connection to the Divine. And the core of that connection is love and joy and gratitude. Understanding this means you shift your focus from the importance of your routine human existence and place it within the context of your Divine nature and experience.

Keep this in focus and the world around you changes. Not just the events that happen to you, but the meaning of the events that you experience.

Begin by asking yourself, *What would it be like if I began to connect to the spiritual part of me? What does a spiritual experience look like for me? How can I connect with the Divine?* These questions can help you think about your own spiritual path:

- What feeds my soul?
- What creates for me a sense of peace?
- What reminds me to see and feel love?
- What experiences help me see the vast mystery of life?

We asked women with whom we worked these questions and found a wide array of answers. Some began with meditation, others immediately took a hike in nature, or headed to a museum to see beautiful works of art. Others simply focused their attention on issues bigger than themselves. Still others began to connect with that voice inside their heads that they associated with the Divine by creating a dialogue.

Spirituality 101

Here are some basics that you should know about spirituality:

- Everyone is on a spiritual journey. It is personal and you get to create it by pulling what makes sense toward you.
- You are not alone. There is a universe filled with spirit beings. You have the power to connect with this realm. It is not a realm of fear or evil. It is a realm of pure divine love and goodness. And it is for you to discover and join and be a part of. It is your home.
- Divine love has emissaries in the form of angels or spiritual beings who want to be a part of your life and help you on your journey. Count on them. They will not fail you. Lean on them. They will not abandon you. Trust them. They belong to us and will help us find our way to the Divine.
- Change hinges on your ability to connect. When you connect, you remember that you are a spiritual being on a human experience. When you connect, you return to the love from which we all emerged and through which we are all connected. We are also able to bring that love into the world around us, act on it, and receive it from others. In so doing we are a part of transformation, not just for ourselves but for the world around us.

This might be a good time to include spiritual observations in your healing journal. Every day, make sure to save time to write about what you did that day that was spiritual in some way. There is no right way to do this. Through experimentation, you will find what works best for you. We only want to reinforce that at this stage of your journey as you connect with the Divine, it is important to pay close attention to your energy. You are connecting to pure love. So being in a frame of mind that allows you to hear love will make your connection easier. Also, remember that no request is too small or too big.

ACTIVITY: *Connecting with Angels*

The following is an activity to connect to your angels, spiritual beings that some people find helpful. Most women that we have talked with have a sense that they have always had a guardian angel. This activity allows you to connect to that protective source. If you're not comfortable doing this, just skip the exercise. But keep an open mind and you might be surprised what happens!

1. First, do some breathing and meditation to center yourself. It is hard to hear the Divine voice when what captivates your attention is anxiety, worry, fear, or revenge. Focus yourself by intentionally relaxing your body and clearing your mind. Try imagining a very lovely box. Decorate it with love and care. Open it up and gently place all you worries in the box. Gently and sweetly tell them that they are important and will be taken care of—later. For now, they must stay in the box until you let them out.
2. Next, imagine a bright, white light that wraps you in safety and protection. Then say a prayer for guidance and protection. Your prayer can be as simple as this: "Please hear my prayer and guide me in my connection to You."
3. Next, on a piece of paper write a variation of these words: "Dear Angels, what would you like me to know?"

4. Listen for the response. Write down what you hear in your head. You may find that you hear the voice for a few minutes and then it may stop and start. You may hear a few words and then hear silence. Write down whatever you hear and be patient. During the silence, wait and listen for more.

5. Repeat often! Like any other skill in your life, you must practice this activity to gain proficiency. The more you do it, the more you gain proficiency, and the louder and clearer the voice becomes.

Once you have heard angelic voices or connected to the angel who is yours and yours alone, say thank you. Feeling gratitude is part of that shift, part of our ability to turn down the volume on worry and anxiety and need and turn up the volume on what we have which amplifies abundance, perfection, and connection to the limitless nature of our true selves. Say thank you as a way of concluding your angelic letter writing. But don't end the focus on gratitude! As you move through your day, practice saying "thank you" as much as you can.

ACTIVITY: *Creating a God Box*

Creating a God box is like an affirmation box, but the purpose is a little different. A God box is used to help you let go of things that are keeping you stuck. Find a small, beautiful box that's unique and special to you. When you are having a difficulty, write down a prayer to your higher power asking for help and guidance. Then place it in your God box and let it go. Sometimes all you can do is pray about a situation and ask for help. Practice letting go and trust that help will be forthcoming. Watch for opportunities that offer a chance for you to resolve the situation.

Visualization and Intuition

Visualization is a wonderful way to transport yourself to a spiritual place. During meditation and visualization, you let your mind lead the way. It is a way to custom-design your life trajectory and create the template for where we want to be, how we can get there, and who can help us on the way.

Following are two visualizations that can help. Both remind you that you are not alone. We are in fact a piece of the Divine and as such are worthy of excellent care and love and respect and nurture and guidance. As you meditate, trust your instincts or that small voice in the back of your mind that directs you. Learn to hear it, trust it, and follow its good council. As you do these visualizations, hear that voice and if you wish to change anything, follow your instincts and do it.

Visualization 1: Meet Your Guardian Angel
Close your eyes and get comfortable. Put your hand on your lower abdomen, just below your bellybutton. As you slowly breathe in through your nose, pull your breath all the way down into your belly so that it makes your hand move ever so slightly. Repeat this lower belly breath.

Close your eyes and imagine yourself in a wonderful garden. This garden belongs to you and it is full of your favorite colors. The only things in this garden are those that you allow in. Imagine what is in the garden with you.

- Is it a bird or several birds singing?
- Is it a waterfall?
- Is it stone walls?

Design your garden so that being in it fills you with peace and joy and happiness. Now imagine a beautiful stone path. You begin to follow the path and as you do, you are filled with the beauty of the garden. As you amble along your path, you see before you the most exquisite creature of beauty you have ever imagined. This is your angel, your guardian angel. You have always known this angel, and now you are reuniting. Your angel has something to tell you. What is it? Listen carefully and write the words down in your journal. Know that you can visit this angel whenever you wish. This angel is yours.

Visualization 2: My Animal Teacher

Connecting to animals is another way to find spirituality. This meditation comes to us from Adrienne Gasperoni, Youth and Family Program Director of Turning Point, a domestic violence shelter in Mt. Clemens, Michigan. Again, some women find this very helpful, but it's not a good choice for everyone. Keep an open mind as you read on.

You are walking with bare feet on soft cool grass. You feel the weight of each footstep sink into the cushioned earth below. The breeze is comfortable and you notice it on your shoulders and upper arms. It brings with it the sweet scent of nature and you take a minute to notice that fragrance and enjoy its simple pleasure. You tune in to the sweet sounds of the wind in the leaves of trees and the gentle lilt of birds singing. Up ahead of you, you notice a beautiful door in the middle of a tall, green hedge and you walk toward it.

As you approach, you see that it is very ornately decorated. It fills you with a sense of awe, as if you are discovering a special and secret place that is here just for you. In fact, you see a welcome sign on the door addressed to you. The sign invites you to come in. You pull a key out of your pocket and unlock the door. You step through the door and lock it behind you. You are in a hallway that leads to another door. You know that behind that next door is the place where your animal waits to greet you. You feel completely safe, because you know that this animal is there to help you reach your highest potential. In fact, you feel very excited. As you walk down the hall you notice that it is decorated in your favorite soft colors and you know it was created just for you.

You approach the second door, reach out, and turn the handle. Every moment in this place is so detailed and alive. You notice the quality of the door handle and really sense the weight of the door as you push it open. You walk in and look around. You see something in the distance and approach it. It is your animal teacher. You have always had a sense that this animal was yours, that this animal guided and protected you. You greet each other with the comfort of old friends.

Ask your animal to help you on your journey. Your animal says it has a gift for you. Magically, a gift, wrapped in beautiful paper, appears in your hands. You gently unwrap it and behold a special gift just for you. You thank your animal guide for the gift and ask if it has any special messages for you right now. After you have heard the message, you turn and walk back toward the door you came in. Open the door and walk into the hall. Pass through the hall and take the key out of your pocket and unlock the next door. As you leave, you lock the door behind you. Know you can return to this place to visit anytime you want to visit your animal guide.

Understanding Animal Guides

Animal guides are special, because their meanings run very deep. If you were able to connect with an animal guide in the previous visualization, ask yourself these questions:

- What animal did you find waiting for you?
- What did the animal say to you?
- How does this message help you?
- What was your gift?
- Why do you suppose your animal gave you this gift?

Now that you have a specific animal to focus on, it's time to study what makes this animal unique and the qualities that help it to thrive in life. Write down the name of the animal you saw, then make a list of all the characteristics you know or think about this animal, for example:

PANTHER
- Big cat
- Black
- Sleek
- Nocturnal
- Large paws
- Graceful
- Quiet
- Eats meat
- Stalks its prey
- Skilled hunter

- Powerful
- Retractable claws
- Mysterious/ Mystical
- Stealthy
- Fast
- Strong
- Independent

As you can see, the example list has qualities that are both objective and subjective. You could take your research a step further on this animal by using materials from the Internet or library. Pay attention to details, including its food sources, if it's a pack animal or solitary, and its natural habitat. Expand your research to include any attributes groups of people have given the animal (you can search online for "panther symbolism"). For example, some South American cultures credit the panther as a guardian or protector.

Next, answer the following questions.

- What characteristics do you feel like you share with this animal?
- What qualities would you like to invite more into your life?
- How does the animal make you feel?

ACTIVITY: *Animal Collage*

If you are feeling creative, make a collage to depict different aspects of your animal guide. The finished product can help remind you that as you make monumental changes in your life, you don't do it alone. You have an animal spirit to guide and protect you. Many women find this comforting. Simply cut out and arrange pictures of your totem or guide animal and things that symbolize both yours and your animal's qualities and features. Have fun!

There are a lot of ways to tell your story. One way is to tell a literal story. Another way is through symbols found in metaphors and similes. A metaphor is a figure of speech that implies a comparison between things that seem to have nothing in common. For example, the phrase, "I am a night owl," referring to someone who likes to stay up at night. Or "I am a rock," referring to someone who is steady and solid. Or "You light up my life," referring to someone who brings joy. A simile is a comparison and has the words "like" or "as" in it. For example, "Your brother burps like a hog." Or "Your daughter is as quiet as a mouse." We include this in the spirituality section because we connect to the spiritual world often through symbols, similes, and metaphors. These parts of speech direct our attention to several things simultaneously—to the literal meaning and to the symbolic meaning something holds. When we compare God to a parent, we are using a metaphor that at once comments on the nature of the Divine and calls our attention to something very earthly.

   Now it is time to think about yourself and the comparisons you would like to make for yourself about yourself. Use metaphors or similes. Be as creative as you can be. Convey to someone who may not know you, who you are; the very heart of you; the core of you.

After you have written them here, it is time to write them on sticky notes or put them on a collage. Bring your inner child and the part of you longing to be silly and laugh to this activity.

Try this activity as a way of continuing to get comfortable tooting your own horn, so to speak. It is important. After all, you are the most wonderful, creative, most unique you we know!

Start like this:

I am a . . . (use a metaphor—make a comparison between yourself and something that has the same qualities as you)

_____

_____

I (put an action word here, for example, eat, work, love) . . . like a . . . (use a simile—make a comparison)

_____

_____

Marking Change Through Ritual

Whether in organized religion or a looser sense of spirituality, rituals are important components of connecting with others. A ritual is an established and often public behavior like a ceremony that marks an event or commemorates a change. We have rituals like birthday cakes with candles on them to celebrate turning another year older. At that ritual, we often invite people we know and like or make sure to include family, have a cake, sing a song, and blow out the candles. Some sources say that this birthday practice can be traced back to Ancient Rome, when candles were used to honor the gods. Others say that the rising smoke takes our wishes to God. The important thing about this ritual is that it marks a specific event, it is public, and it lets others in our social world know that we have changed. We have become a year older and socially, that may have many implications. For example, it may mean you are old enough to drive or vote, or too old to be single! The meaning is socially created and recognized and people treat us accordingly.

The Importance of Sharing Rituals

When you move from an abusive relationship and do the work of healing it is possible that the people in your social world will change as you change. We tend to attract those to us whose energy most resembles ours. Whether those around you have been on the whole journey with you or whether they are people you have only recently met, you need to mark your own shifts and changes and do so publicly.

Both of us teach at a university and regularly participate in graduations. When students ask us whether they should participate, we always answer with a resounding, "Yes!" Seldom do our students have the same friends they came to campus with when they graduate. But they need to proclaim to family and friends that they have reached a point of change. They are no longer "students," they are now "graduates." As graduates, there are different expectations for their behavior and different expectations for how they should be treated. As graduates, they have a new social status. If they miss the ritual, they fail to honor the hard work that brought them to the changes they experienced and cheat themselves out of public recognition for the changes. The same is true for you and your healing journey!

ACTIVITY: *Change and Growth*

For a moment, let's take inventory. There may be plenty of things you still want to change in your life, even if you've come a long way since leaving a violating relationship. We are, after all, always growing and changing and becoming. This constant change process or even goal orientation doesn't mean, however, that you shouldn't stop and take stock of where you are and what you have accomplished. Especially when this signifies a change in status.

This activity will help you see where and when you have changed. It should take about twenty minutes, so give yourself ample time. This activity works best by using three different color index cards. But you can easily improvise here by using any paper you have and coloring the margin of the paper a different color or using different colored pens. You will need three colors.

This activity marks your turning points from Victim, to Survivor, to Thriver. If you are using three different colors of index cards, designate one the color you will use to describe what happened in your life when you were a Victim. Write down several key life events, one event per card. Next, use another color set of cards and write down what happened in your life when you were surviving. Again, generally write one life event per card. Finally, choose a third color and designate it your

Thriver cards. What happened, is happening, or will happen in this stage of your life?

After you have recorded several events and are all finished, lay the cards out on the table or floor in such a way as to reflect your journey. Your arrangement might be linear, or circular, or all over the place! Whatever makes sense to you is how you should arrange your cards. The arrangement should tell the story of your journey through time and through healing. If you haven't gotten to where you want to be as a Thriver yet, that's fine. Simply record where you are going as life events on an index card and arrange it in the array.

Where You've Been

Next, let's take stock of all the amazing changes you've made. Try answering these questions to help you.

- What patterns do you see?
- What seemed to be the impetus for some major life changes? In other words, what helped you or spurred you on toward change?
- What marked your transition from Victim to Survivor? In other words how did you know you moved from one stage to another?
- What marked your transition from Survivor to Thriver?
- What changes are you most proud of?
- What changes were the hardest to make?
- What work lies ahead and how does it feel?

Whether you have arrived "there," at that perfect place in your life, or whether you still have work to do, it is important to look ahead and see the wonderful things that are on your own horizon. It is important also to know that you can get there.

The changes in status you are marking through this activity are changes that would be aided through a ritual that tells the world that you are a changed woman who must now be treated differently.

Create a Thriver Ritual

When you were in the Victim stage you needed certain things—for example, emergency housing and medical treatment. When you were in the Survivor stage, you might have needed legal consultation and a more long-term housing plan. Because you needed certain things, the world around you provided you with those things or treated you according to your needs. As you head into Thriver mode, however, you require different things and the world around you must treat you differently based on those needs. A ritual is a way to mark—really to publicly declare—those changes and to allow the world around you to see and treat you differently based on the changes you identify.

So now is the time to create your Thriver ritual. What will it be and who will be a part of it? For a moment, just let your mind wander to see yourself center stage, letting the world know you have become someone and something different than when you began your journey.

Building a Ritual

As you envision the perfect ritual, here are some things to keep in mind.

- Rituals are events that are out of the ordinary. They are special and might include an action or way of doing things that you may not likely repeat in everyday life.
- Rituals are public. They announce to the society in which you live that you are changed. This doesn't have to be *all* of society, but it should include the society that is important to you—those people with whom you interact on a regular basis.
- Rituals should relate to the event you are marking. They often hold some symbolic value. For example, when we graduate, we walk across a stage symbolizing the transition or journey we have made from student to graduate. A group of women Danielle worked with conducted a ritual at the head of a bridge and each woman walked across to the applause of her groupmates to mark that they had become something different.

So what might be a good ritual for you and who will you include? Who is in the community that you would like to invite and surround yourself with?

Part of the Future Is Letting Go of the Past: Forgiveness

We wanted to make sure we included forgiveness and letting go as part of every woman's spiritual development.

Here is why. Everyone, and we mean *everyone*, has moments or times in their life that they are not proud of, that they wish they had done better, that they simply regret. Understanding this as a human phenomenon is important. It is the price of living. How you deal with these moments is also very important. If you can learn from them, integrate what you have learned into new behavior so you don't have to repeat the same life lessons and move on, then you are evidencing healing.

Too often, we hold on to these failures or regrets as shame. But shame does nothing for us in terms of helping us change. In fact, it often does the opposite; it paralyzes. And when we are paralyzed, we cannot learn or change or grow. So it is important to face the worst and figure out where to go from there.

Self-forgiveness is part of spirituality because when we connect to divine love, even those things that we did that were huge failings—are loved. As such, they are a part of all of us and a part of the Divine. Shame does not help you. It simply makes you feel bad and makes connecting to the Divine love difficult. Things that make you feel bad are those things that you try to avoid. If you tend to lock shameful things away in a dark corner of your mind, they will only grow and fester. Love puts things in the light, where they can be worked with and understood.

Mistakes Are Okay

We promise you that you won't get everything right in your life. You won't always say what you want to say. You won't always do the right thing. And when that happens know that that is part of being human. We all make mistakes. It is okay. The most important thing is to learn from them and you can't learn from them when your mistakes are shrouded in shame. Identify that voice in your own mind that shames you when you make a mistake. Talk to it. Tell it that you appreciate its concern but you no longer need it. Tell it too that you are human and will make mistakes. And you accept your mistakes as opportunities for growth and change. Alcoholics Anonymous has an aphorism that says, "We are as sick as our secrets." Our mistakes become toxic when they become secrets hidden away in our minds, shrouded in shame. Don't let your mistakes become your secrets. Tell someone about them, if for no other reason than to make sure they do not become toxic. And then put it to rest. Know that when you make a mistake, very seldom is it a forever mistake. And most of the time it can be remedied or worked out. And that kind of work is good work!

ACTIVITY: *Self-Forgiveness*

Instead of writing down a behavior or a choice you made that needs forgiveness, hold it instead in your mind. See it, feel it, know that it was you making the best choice you could at the time, even if it inflicted pain on others. Now, see it through the eyes of love. See yourself in that moment through the eyes of love.

See yourself in that moment or time of your life and say these words to the mental picture of you: *I love you. I forgive you. I let you go.* See yourself and others who are in the picture surrounded by white light of love and forgiveness. Fill your heart with love and forgiveness. Looking at yourself, repeat the words, *I love you, I forgive you, and I let you go.* Watch the image get very, very small. It is a tiny ball of white light. You pick it up and very carefully hold it.

Now envision a beautiful angel, animal guide, or other spiritual being standing next to you. It is the most magnificent creature you have ever seen. It knows you and loves you. Hand the ball of white light to the being and know that those inside the ball will be loved and cared for, nurtured and forgiven.

This activity also works well when we have angry feelings toward someone. If you are holding on to angry feelings and you can't seem to shake them, they are preventing you from getting on with the business of creating a positive and happy and successful life for yourself. After all, you can't be invested in negativity like anger, hatred, and thoughts of revenge while you create a positive life built around love, joy, and forgiveness.

Wrapping It All Up

The most important thing to know about spirituality is that you are not alone. You are surrounded by loving beings who know you and love you and want you to succeed in everything that you do. You can grow in your understanding of them merely by turning your attention to them and asking to hear their voices.

When you approach yourself with love and care and treat others through that love, what you reflect is reflected back to you. When you give yourself room to grow and to be human, you give others that same room and you join with them in a shared journey. This helps you create the community you want to draw around you. By drawing to you the community you want to engage with, you change your world. Yes, you are just that powerful. Hold on to that knowledge. You are that powerful. Your power is bolstered by a whole host of helpful heavenly beings who are on your side and helping you create a better world.

Earlier in this book, we told you that the wounds of violation change us forever. You are and have been forever changed by your experiences. But think of it this way. While it may sound like a cliché, it is these experiences that make us who we are and who we can become. Peter Levine, author of *Waking the Tiger: Healing Trauma,* echoes this sentiment when he suggests "Of all the maladies that attack the human organism, trauma may ultimately be one that is recognized as beneficial. . . . because in the healing of trauma, a transformation takes place—one that can improve the quality of life."

This book has not only been a process in learning new skills that can improve the quality of your life, but it has also been an exercise in unlearning the realities you accepted as a victim of violation. It has also lead you through a process to reconnect with your true, amazing, and wonderful self. We also hope you got the chance to reconnect with your dreams and to expand and amplify them to create a clear path into your wonderful and fulfilled future. At the end of every journey a new one begins . . .

Looking Ahead

It is time for you to feel proud of all you have accomplished and the ways you have grown in completing this Rite of Passage. It is natural to feel scared and excited as you let go of the past and look forward to the future. You might not yet know your final destination, or who you will ultimately become as you continue to grow and change.

Sometimes you grow and change most when things are the most difficult for you. Easy times do not force us to be strong and to keep going when we are discouraged. We all like comfort and peace, but it is in the moments of chaos that we must find the calm in our self and spirit to find a way out of the chaos.

Moments of Doubt

As you navigate your path, there may be times when you may feel a little wobbly in the creation process. That is okay. Take it one step at a time. Revisit the activities in this book as much as you wish to. Like loving friends, these activities will welcome you back for a visit and a refresher whenever you need them. They are here for you. And as you blaze your new life path, you may wish to revisit the activities in this book because your perspective will change and grow and you may find the truths you hold will change and grow, too. You may find that you will experience the activities differently at different times in your life.

Enjoy Your Community and Help Others

Keep in touch with other women. Find a place for spiritual worship if that is a comfort to you. Try to set aside time to meditate daily or for some quiet time for just you. Expect every relationship, not just those with men, to be based on respect and mutual caring and empathy. Jealousy and possessiveness are not healthy and are often warning signs of potential abuse.

The twelfth step in the recovery movement states that "Having had a spiritual awakening as the result of these steps, we tried to carry this message to alcoholics and to practice these principles in all our affairs." Modify this a little bit for your situation. Having become stronger spiritually, and having grown as a woman, you should practice honesty, respect, and dignity in your all relationships and help other women who may be struggling whenever the opportunity arises. And you should expect the same from others.

You're in Charge

Remember, you are in charge. You are in control of you, your future, and your destiny. Throughout this book you created and called the shots. And you take that knowledge, wisdom, and perspective into the future.

In creating your future, you will expand the hope and wisdom and strength that is already a part of you and create a limitless world for yourself and your loved ones. It is there. Believe it. It belongs to you.

The last most important thing for you to know is that you are a powerful, wonderful woman with the ability to create the world you want to have.

A Time to Reflect

Reflection on the steps we take toward Thriving is important. By frequently taking stock of the changes you are making, you can be mindful of the changes that intentionally come from you and are becoming a part of you. You call the shots for this leg of your life journey. Though you want to focus on moving forward, stopping to look at the progress you've made is a great way to celebrate your successes and identify your next steps.

Reflecting on the changes you have made so far is an important step in recognizing those thoughts and beliefs that are new to you. It also helps as a benchmark on your journey.

ACTIVITY: *Reflecting*

Think back on the activities you completed in this unit to discover which has been the most helpful for you. Can you put into words why it was helpful? Recognizing what helped you make important changes means that you can focus on that piece to help you make future changes. You might also reflect on the transformation you have experienced in your life right now and celebrate it.

What has changed for you?

_____

_____

_____

_____

_____

What new picture or image of yourself is emerging?

_____

_____

_____

_____

_____

How have your thoughts changed?

_____

_____

_____

_____

_____

What has changed in your living, work, or family environment? For example, did you get a job? Do you have a new place to live?

_____

_____

_____

_____

_____

What activities do you want to repeat and why?

_____

_____

_____

_____

Which activity taught you the most about yourself?

_____

_____

_____

_____

_____

How might you celebrate or mark the changes you've made
so far?

_____

_____

_____

_____

_____

A Plan for Continued Healing

*"If you can dream it, you can see it.
If you can see, it you can get there."*

In this unit, you will:

- Learn more about the relationship between your thoughts and your capacity to alter your life as part of identity construction and healing work
- While keeping your positive focus, you will plan for some "bumps in the road" in your positivity
- Develop strategies for handling issues and problems that might arise while staying true to your new self

Reflecting on the Past to Create Your Future

One thing we hear from women who are healing and trying to create positive thoughts is that the world intervenes with negativity and they can wind up feeling derailed from the healing journey. One way to handle that derailment is to go back through this book and review and perhaps redo those activities that helped you the most. Another thing to do is to explore all the healing opportunities we've offered, even the ones you didn't immediately connect with. And a third is to understand a little more the relationship between your thoughts and the reality you are creating.

"Stand at the edge of the water," anthropologist Colin Turnbull wrote in 1983, capturing the words of an Mbuti guide, "and look at your reflection. Who is it? It looks like you, but its head is down there, looking up at the other you. Is it thinking the same thing, wondering who you are? Then put your foot over the water and gently lower it. The other foot will come up to meet yours, and if you are very careful not to break the surface of the water, you will feel the other foot touch yours. You are getting to know your other self."

Turnbull worked with Pygmies living in the Ituri forest in Zaire. Danielle found this quote shortly before completing her doctorate in anthropology and it impressed her because it serves as a metaphor for the way people create identity. It reminded her that as *changing agents,* we must constantly take stock of who we are and who we are becoming and as we change we must come to know all iterations of our selves. When we heal, we become something new. We also retain the memory and knowledge of where we have been. Thus there are several "me-s" that we must make sure we know and incorporate. As a metaphor it also suggests that identity is a reflected process. What can emerge in this reflection are sometimes two different images of the same person.

When Danielle was researching the lives of women who had made enormous changes and had moved away from violation, she heard them refer to their experience with violation in very similar ways. These women consistently said, "in my former life" or "in my past life." That is, they made a distinction between the happiness they had created in the present life and the past trauma they had endured. These women educated us about the steps women took to create and rebuild their lives.

But think about their statements in light of the Turnbull quote. It is as though women saw two separate selves at two very distinct periods in their lives. Sometimes we change so much that we can barely recognize the women we were say, five or ten years ago. We believed things and acted in ways that we could never do again. And so the reference to the past as a separate person makes sense. But we have found that it is important for these selves to stay in touch with each other—especially in the beginning stages of healing. Because sometimes the things we have experienced through violation can cause little hiccups that we want to be prepared for.

Part of your work as you heal is to understand the change process while we build a perfect and joy-filled life. As discussed in Healing Unit 3, this is joyful work. It is also work that takes practice and that can come in fits and starts. As you have moved through the activities in this book, you have learned a number of skills that help you shift your thinking about who you are and what you can expect from the world around you. Let's now look at the long-term processes for rebuilding identity and try some final activities that you can do when issues, problems, or conflicts arise.

The Problem with Movies and Scripts

Neurobiologists like Rick Hanson, author of *Buddha's Brain*, tell us that the brain is hardwired to help us recognize and think through danger or threats to our survival. The ability to recognize and respond to danger is a contributing factor for why we have lasted so long as a species. Not only does our brain have the ability to perceive potential threats, but we automatically store that information where it serves as a template for future interactions. Think for a minute about touching something hot as a child like the stove or an iron. We don't do that twice because the brain holds on to that experience and without us doing anything consciously, remembers that hot stoves hurt, and warns us not to do it again. In fact, part of the residue from that experience can be a tinge of anxiety or extra caution around hot surfaces.

We also know that humans perceive and store many more negative experiences than positive ones. Once we have had a negative experience, it takes a lot of positive ones to overcome that one. This survival mechanism can make us anxious and vigilant, quick to sense and react to threat.

This survival mechanism can make you anxious and vigilant, quick to sense and react to threat. This can be hiccup number one. As we heal from violation we have to learn to distinguish genuine threat, a relationship that can really harm us or undermine our sense of self, from a relationship that cannot.

This can be very difficult because a lot of violating men present themselves as caring, concerned, genuine, and attentive only to show their true colors as someone who is frightening, angry, and controlling. We have been taught through violation to mistrust other women as potential rivals or as threats to the private hell many batterers construct for their partners. These past experiences can be scripts or movies that play in our heads reminding us of experiences we have perceived as threats so that we don't run into trouble again. This can be hiccup number two. As we heal, we need to connect with others. We need to intentionally change the script that we hear. This will have to be an ongoing and overt practice until it becomes natural. We had practiced doing this in Healing Unit 4 when we listened to the voices that played in our heads about ourselves. Now it is time to expand that activity and listen to the voices that play in our heads about others.

We are also hard wired to think in terms of fight or flight, friend or foe. This is a protective mechanism that we carry with us from the earliest days of mankind. But, we are no longer the hunters and gatherers of the plains and our lives and relationships are much more complicated. As you move forward in creating your new future, be aware of these instinctive reactions to fight or run away. As we heal, we may have an empty place inside for a long time that comes from not getting the love and praise we deserved from the people we loved. This makes us vulnerable to "flee" into the arms of someone who appears to offer us the love we crave to fill the empty space we carry.

In Healing Unit 5, Danielle told about a group of women with whom she worked who really hated their caseworker. They complained about her quite a bit. Yet as they thought through her characteristics, they began to see that she was a complicated person. And though some of the things she did and the way she did them really upset the women working with her, they also saw that part of being upset was a reaction to their experiences with power and control in their past. By talking about their feelings and the gut "alerts" they heard inside their own heads they were able to sort out what traits actually belonged to the case worker and which issues belonged to them.

ACTIVITY: *Thought Catching and Stopping*

When you are in a new situation, be prepared for triggers or unfamiliar conditions that can provoke the fight/flight, or as Karen calls it, the potential "fleeing into the arms of a (any) waiting man" response. Pay attention to your external surroundings and make a conscious note of the people, sounds, and activities going on around you. Then turn your attention inward and monitor your own physical, emotional, and cognitive reactions. Are you tensing up? Are you looking down or ahead? Are you moving forward or stuck? What are you feeling? What do your feelings and physical reactions tell you about the situation? What choices do you want to make?

The point here is to catch the reaction before you react. Remember, we are hard wired to react with fight or flight, and as you heal, you want to have more choices open to you in order to create the future you want for yourself. As you tune into your reaction, think it through. Ask yourself, what do I want for myself? Is this the place I want to be in? If so, take a deep breath, pull up your strength, and go forward. If you are not ready, or if your instincts are warning you this is not a good situation, calmly remain in control and remove yourself.

When we are trying to stop the instant reaction and tune into the feeling so we can process it, we can use a visual cue or physical cue to help us. Sometimes visualizing a stop sign is enough to give us pause while we think things through. Think, "stop" and imagine a stop sign right in the center of your mind. Breathe and slow down.

Another technique is to wear a rubber band around your wrist and snap it (not too hard!) when you find yourself reacting. It sounds silly, but the physical sting distracts you for a moment, enabling you to come back in control. And, the sting also provides negative reinforcement, eventually discouraging you from reacting in anger or fear when you don't want to.

Remember to use your journal when you are working through these kinds of things. This will help you identify patterns so that you can take these small events and make larger changes in your life.

ACTIVITY: *Sorting Through a Threat and the Reaction*

This activity builds on the one you did earlier, in Healing Unit 4. Think for a minute about a relationship with a person in your life who represents an authority figure. This is someone who has power over you in some way—it could be a professor, a boss, a landlord, or a caseworker.

Take a piece of paper and divide it in half. On the top of the left-hand side, write down this statement: "When people have power over me I tend to . . ." Think about the range of reactions you have to those in power over you. List as many as you can. What differences do you see?

Now, on the right-hand side of the paper, start teasing out the differences. What causes one reaction from you, like being overly nice, from another in which you simply want to run away? What is the difference? On the right-hand side of the page at the top write this statement: "I do this when I feel . . ."

When you are finished see if you can evaluate your "hot spots" or situations that might cause you to react strongly. These are reactions that you will want to know about. These reactions may be perfectly suited to the situation. Or they can constitute areas where you might react in a way that no longer fits the current situation. Either way, it is important information for you to have because it allows you to decide how you want to react. It also allows you to ask the question, *Is this a hot stove that can hurt me or is this my memory of a hot stove and is this now something different?*

Change the Channel and Get a New Movie

We all encounter relationships that contain discord. We have found in our work with women that as they heal that it can be very difficult to keep positive and joyful when these relationships push their way to the front and center of our psyches. We have heard women say it is hard to stay positive when "X" happens. So here is what we want you to know. When you have been violated, you can respond to discord or tension strongly. Because of your past experiences with violation, it often doesn't take much to trigger feelings and reactions from the past. It is very natural to play a movie in your minds about the discord over and over again. In part, it makes you feel better. It is a little like nursing a wound. And in part it is your brain's way of reinforcing "hot stove" experiences.

But as you heal, you really need to interrupt the movies that show you as a victim or even as a struggling survivor. You have to create new movies in the present moment where you can continuously see yourself as a Thriver—in spite of tensions or problems.

Remember, no one has the right to hurt you. So changing the movie is *not* about finding ways to put up with a bad situation. In fact, changing the movie can help you find your path away from a bad situation.

In the previous chapter, we talked about the importance of taking stock of those changes, noting them, and celebrating them even when the change process is incomplete or even when you haven't yet reached the Thriving stage all the way. The importance of recognizing and celebrating those changes is that they become a part of you through your vision. When you see the changes you have made, stop and really see them, they become real for you. They become a part of your implicit memories and no one can take them away from you. As memory, they form the templates for future changes that your brain uses to help you anticipate the world and navigate your environment.

Keep Finding the Positive

Neurobiologists like Rick Hanson also tell us that much of the reality we experience is manufactured reality. It is a simulation made of pieces of information—often quite incomplete pieces. And our brains fill in the gaps. Since trauma has taught you to construct the world based on very frightening pieces of reality, it is so important as you heal to continue to build a repertoire of very positive, healthy, and compassionate memories.

Seeing the positive does something else. It creates a reality in and for your brain that can indeed shape future thoughts and guide your behavior.

Healing is all about changing your thinking. By changing your thinking, you relearn yourself and the world around you. That is a wonderful work and no doubt you have learned so much about yourself in this process. You will continue to learn about yourself, to learn and grow and develop in wonderful ways. But when you heal, you not only relearn who you are, you actually reinvent who you are. So you not only reinvent yourself, but you literally reinvent the world.

This last concept—reinventing the world—is not an easy one to grasp, for several reasons. One reason is that it defies the logic you have been taught—after all, how many times have you been told that the world does not change for you, that you must change to fit into the world?

But it's time to call that belief into question. When you change the way you think, you actually change who you are, and thus you indeed do change the world around you. This is important because as you continue your journey, you will be confronted by less-than-positive people, people who want to suck you back into negative relationships, or who see you as a projection of their own negative thoughts and issues. You may also find that you are often combating your own tendencies to think negatively or to engage in disaster thinking.

Reimagining Negative Experiences

Being aware of these potential difficulties can help you create a contingency plan of sorts. For example, like a lot of us, Danielle has a tendency to focus on interactions with people when they didn't go well. She turns them over and over in her mind, trying to see how they could have gone better. This is a good quality—in part. But it has its negative side too. Focusing too long on those interactions makes them very important. It expands them and makes them larger than they were. It also doesn't always allow for a solution because ultimately it culminates in worry. This pattern is in part informed by experiences with a hot stove. When this pattern starts for her, she has learned to stop the movie, and play the solution. She asks herself, what do you want to have happen here? What is the best possible scenario? Do you remember when we asked you to hold up a stop sign in your mind to stop negative thinking? This is similar—but we want you to go a step further. Create an action plan and then implement it. For Danielle, she stops the negative movie and creates a new one. She plays out the best scenario that could happen and actually feels those feelings instead. She takes time to savor the feelings. Then she implements the scenes in the "movie."

Recently, Danielle felt she slighted a colleague at a meeting by not remembering her name. She stopped the negative movie—in which the colleague hated her forever—and created a new one. She explained to the colleague that remembering names was difficult for her and she had meant no slight. In the movie, the colleague smiled and said thank you. Danielle felt relieved and grateful. In "real time," Danielle then used the movie to help her take corrective action. She sent her colleague a funny card recalling the slight and apologizing. In real life, her colleague called her, said she hadn't even noticed the slight, but was delighted to get the card and touched that someone actually cared so much about her feelings. Win/win! When Danielle thinks about this colleague, she takes out the "good" movie—the positive scenario that really happened—and replays it.

Finding the Good Everywhere

There might be times when you can't see the best possible outcome. Life is complex! Sometimes you know you want a situation to change, but you just don't know how or what you want to happen. That can generate a lot of anxiety and can keep you stewing, creating movies that have no good ending.

One possible solution draws from Healing Unit 6 Simply ask the Universe or God or the angels to see your situation and help to bring about the best possible solution for everyone involved. Then feel the feelings of resolution. *Know* that the situation will be taken care of by a power bigger than you. Make a mental note of the day and time and see yourself saying, "Whew! What a relief that that is now taken care of!" Make sure that you do not revisit the old movies. Revisit instead the sense of relief that the situation will work out well.

You don't just have to think about those problems that are happening in real time. This is where metaphors can come in quite handy too. Metaphors allow you to have the positive feelings without revisiting a troubling situation. Here is how it works. Our brains do not distinguish between a literal event and a metaphorical event. In fact, several studies show that the brain can be intentionally tricked into conflating reality, for example, something that is physically heavy, with a metaphor or a symbolic representation, a book that is important—i.e., weighty. So we can use metaphor to help us re-create the movies that play in our heads about conflict or tension.

We worked with a woman in one of our healing groups who had a tough situation at her job. She wasn't being fulfilled by her work and she was frequently challenged by coworkers who questioned how she completed her work. She shared with the group that she was not happy and did not know how to fix the situation. She felt her work unhappiness was impeding her healing because she focused on the negative and had a hard time seeing the positive or good things in her life. She could recount the positive things in her life, but could not stay in a joyful place because she was troubled by her job.

Rather than dissecting the interactions at work, we suggested she try the following activities as a way of helping her create a new movie. The new movies can help you create new solutions, too. When you hit rough patches in your relationships while you are healing, rather than respond defensively (an old pattern) you are working to respond in a new way, by seeing the positive and responding with love, compassion, empathy, and joy. Empathy for others begins with empathy for yourself. And the ability to respond in this way begins by creating a good memory of that response. In a way, you are creating positive memories for your brain through these active daydreams. They needn't last more than a few seconds. But they can create powerful and positive templates for future responses.

ACTIVITY: *Active Daydream: Setting My Table*

This is an imagining activity—an active daydream. You can do it anywhere, but we recommend for the first time that you do it like a meditation. So get comfortable. Silence your distractions—turn off the phone, radio, TV. Take four or five breaths to help you relax and get focused.

Now, imagine that you are in a lovely room. It is a room that you really want to spend time in because it is just so beautiful. Really see that room. See all of its nooks and crannies. See where light shines in. What does it feel like to be in this room? Where do you feel these feelings?

In the center of the room is a long table. Your task is to set this table in the most beautiful and pleasing way you can. In order to get supplies for your table, all you have to do is to imagine them. There are no limits to what you can try. If one tablecloth doesn't seem right, change it by imagining a different one. Don't stop until the table is set and is absolutely radiant. What feelings does this image conjure up for you? What does it feel like to look at your handiwork? What does it feel like to look at something so wonderful and beautiful and inviting?

Now, think about who would you like to be invited to this table and how would you like them to behave. Can you see them? As each person you invite appears at the table, they are smiling and grateful. They radiate love toward you. They appreciate what you have done for them. They admire your handiwork. Feel those feelings. You are loved and admired and adored. Does someone at the table stand up and make a speech about you? Do you stand up and make a speech? What is said?

How would you like to conclude this daydream? Does everyone eat together? Or is it enough just to share this moment?

As you conclude your daydream, see each person look directly at you with love and admiration. They see your talent and skill and competence. They know who you are. Each person at the table says, thank you to you.

Following is another activity that can help with tough relationship issues. Rather than letting them pause or derail your healing, here is another way to move through them. This activity too starts on the metaphorical level. It involves showing tenderness and understanding and compassion to yourself, and developing expertise in empathy and active response. When you are open to yourself and your own subjectivity, and can show kindness, forgiveness, and love to yourself, you can be open to showing those emotions to others.

ACTIVITY: *Active Daydream: Loving Kindness*

Here is another activity that can help with tough relationship issues that may emerge in your path. Rather than let them derail your healing, or even pause your healing, here is another way to move through them. This activity too starts on the metaphorical level. It involves showing tenderness and understanding and compassion to yourself. It also involves developing expertise in empathy and active response. When you are open to yourself and your own subjectivity, and can show kindness and forgiveness and love to yourself, you can be open to showing those emotions to others.

A national science association has notified you that they have created a clone of you. The clone is now a tiny baby. The chair of the association asks you to be the mother to this baby because you know exactly what this baby will need; you know the kindness, love, tenderness, and affection this baby will want and require. You accept the offer and are handed the most beautiful baby you have ever seen wrapped in a soft and fuzzy blanket. You are thrilled to hold this wonderful baby. Can you feel that joy? Can you feel the sense of awe and wonder and excitement?

The baby begins to cry. You are not alarmed; instead, you are confident. You know exactly why baby-you is crying and you are quick with the remedy. The baby stops crying and smiles her gratitude at you. You feel so proud to be able to take care of another human so effectively. You feel proud that you were able to empathize with this baby-you. The chair of the science association thanks you for being so compassionate and in tune with the baby's needs. You respond by saying that you love this baby and know just what this baby needs. You feel connected to this baby. You feel confident and grateful and important.

Keep What Works Working

Few skills in life ever stick unless they are practiced. And so changing your thinking requires constant monitoring and vigilance. We all have our areas that can be Achilles heels. It is important to recognize those areas, keep them in check, and keep building new skills that allow you to continue on your healing trajectory.

You may have heard the saying, old habits die hard. There is a reason for this. When you think a certain way, you develop pathways in your brain that are like train tracks. The more we think certain thoughts, the more the train tracks are worn, the deeper the grooves become, the easier it is for the train to follow the tracks. The work of healing involves creating new tracks, new grooves.

But you can easily fall back into the old way of doing things—the old way of thinking, and being—because those grooves are well worn and because these patterns are familiar. Acknowledging this is important. Integrating the activities we have covered in this book into your daily life is equally important, as is continuing the opportunities for your own healing.

We recommend the following ways to continue your work.

1. End each day with a gratitude prayer. It can be as short or as long as you wish and the only requirement is for you to *feel* what it is you are grateful for. It can be as big as a bonus you got at work or as small as a good parking place.
2. Begin each day with a love-based mantra. It can be long or short. The object is to feel love for yourself, your family, your coworkers, your nation, your world.
3. Create rituals that mark special moments. Many women we have worked with light a candle to signify a moment in which they have had a success. Don't save these moments or postpone the celebration. Celebrate them as they come.
4. Keep learning about yourself and your needs and your path. To help you we have created a list of books in the

following appendix that can keep you learning new things, creating new feelings, and making new movies about who you are and the wonderful journey you are on!

A final word: You are not the abuse. It does not define you; it does not own you. It is not who you are. There are so many parts to who you are, so many good things, that even when you say you are a Thriver or Survivor, you are still giving the abuse too much space in who you are. You are here for a reason and the world needs you to be fully who you are, unbound by events out of your control. Even though it took great courage to leave, leaving the abuse is not and will not be your greatest accomplishment in life. Your greatest accomplishment in life is having the courage to be you.

Appendix

Additional Resources

Andrews, Ted (1993). *Animal-Speak: The Spiritual & Magical Powers of Creatures Great & Small*. Woodbury, MN: Llewellyn.

Armstrong, Jennifer (1998). *Pockets*. New York: Crown.

Arrien, Angeles (1993). *The Four-Fold Way*. New York: Harper

Baba, Sri Sathya Sai (1984). *Bhagavad Gita*. Tustin, CA: Sathya Sai Book Center of America.

Booris-Dunchunstand, Eileen (2007). *Finding Forgiveness: A 7-Step Program for Letting Go of Anger and Bitterness*. New York: McGraw-Hill.

Brach, Tara (2004). *Radical Acceptance—Embracing Your Life With the Heart of a Buddha*. New York: Bantam.

Bradley, Marion Zimmer (1982). *The Mists of Avalon*. New York: Ballantine.

Canfield, Jack, and Mark Victor Hansen (1993). *Chicken Soup for the Soul*. Deerfield Beach, FL: Health Communications.

Carnes, Robin Deen, and Sally Craig (1998). *Sacred Circles—A Guide to Creating Your Own Women's Spirituality Group*. New York: HarperCollins.

Cheung, Monit (2006). *Therapeutic Games and Guided Imagery*. Chicago: Lyceum.

Chodron, Pema (1997). *When Things Fall Apart—Heart Advice for Difficult Times*. Boston: Shambhala.

Chopra, Deepak (1994). *The Seven Spiritual Laws of Success*. San Rafael, CA: Amber-Allen and New World Library.

Dabholkar, Govind Raghunath (2002). *The Wonderful Life and Teachings of Shri Sai Baba*. Mumbai: D. M. Sukthankar.

Dalai Lama and Howard C. Cutler (1998). *The Art of Happiness*. New York: Penguin.

Diamont, Anita (1997). *The Red Tent*. New York: Picador.

Dyer, Wayne (2009). *Excuses Begone!: How to Change Lifelong Self-Defeating Thinking Habits*. Carlsbad, CA: Hay House.

——— (2004). *The Power of Intention*. Carlsbad, CA: Hay House.

Fischer, Kay-Laurel, and Michael F. McGrane (1997). *Journey Beyond Abuse—A Step-by-Step Guide to Facilitating Women's Domestic Abuse Groups*. St. Paul, MN: Amherst H. Wilder Foundation.

Frasier, Debra (1991). *On the Day You Were Born*. New York: Harcourt Brace

Gangaji (2005). *The Diamond in Your Pocket: Discovering Your True Radiance*. Boulder, CO: Sounds True.

Gilbert, Elizabeth (2006). *Eat, Pray, Love*. New York: Viking.

Ginolfi, Arthur (1989). *The Tiny Star*. New York: Checkerboard.

Goble, Paul (1984). *Buffalo Woman*. New York: Aladdin.

Helmstetter, Shad (1982). *What to Say When You Talk to Yourself*. Scottsdale, AZ: Grindle.

Hesse, Hermann (1951). *Siddhartha*. New York: Bantam.

Hicks, Esther and Jerry (2006). *The Amazing Power of Deliberate Intent: Living the Art of Allowing*. Carlsbad, CA: Hay House.

——— (2009). *The Vortex: Where the Law of Attraction Assembles All Cooperative Relationships*. Carlsbad, CA: Hay House.

Kidd, Sue Monk (2002). *The Secret Life of Bees*. New York: Penguin.

Kinsella, Sophie (2001). *Confessions of a Shopaholic*. New York: Dial.

Levine, Peter A. (2005). *Healing Trauma: A Pioneering Program for Restoring the Wisdom of Your Body*. Boulder, CO: Sounds True.

Levitin, Daniel J. (2006). *This Is Your Brain on Music: The Science of a Human Obsession*. New York: Penguin.

Maharshi, Ramana (1985). *Be As Your Are: The Teachings of Sri Ramana Maharshi*. London: Penguin.

Mark, Barbara, and Trudy Griswold (1997). *The Angelspeake Book of Prayer and Healing*. New York: Simon and Schuster.

Moss, Richard (2007). *The Mandala of Being: Discovering the Power of Awareness*. Novato, CA: New World Library.

Nhat Hanh, Thich (1991). *Peace Is Every Step: The Path of Mindfulness in Everyday Life*. New York: Bantam.

Price, John Randolph (1993). *The Angels Within Us*. New York: Random House Ballantine.

Remen, Rachel Naomi (1996). *Kitchen Table Wisdom*. New York: Riverhead.

——— (2000). *My Grandfather's Blessing*. New York: Riverhead.

Renard, Gary (2002). *The Disappearance of the Universe: Straight Talk About Illusions, Past Lives, Religion, Sex, Politics, and the Miracles of Forgiveness*. Carlsbad, CA: Hay House.

Robbins, Tom (1980). *Still Life with Woodpecker*. New York: Bantam Dell.

Rosenbloom, Dena, and Mary Beth Williams (1999). *Life After Trauma—A Workbook for Healing*. New York: Guilford.

Rothfuss, Patrick (2007). *The Name of the Wind*. New York: DAW.

Ruiz, Don Miguel (1997). *The Four Agreements: A Practical Guide to Personal Freedom*. San Rafael, CA: Amber-Allen.

Sams, Jamie (1993). *The 13 Original Clan Mothers*. New York: HarperCollins.

Spalding, Baird (1924). *Life and Teachings of Masters of the Far East, Volume 1*. San Francisco: California Press.

Stratton, Elizabeth K. (1997). *Seeds of Light—Healing Meditations for Body and Soul*. New York: Fireside.

Svirinskaya, Alla (2005). *Energy Secrets—The Ultimate Well-Being Plan*. Carlsbad, CA: Hay House.

Tolle, Eckhart (2005). *A New Earth: Awakening to Your Life's Purpose*. New York: Penguin.

Vaughn, Frances, and Roger Walsh (1983). *Gifts from a Course in Miracles*. New York: Penguin Putnam.

Veltman, Jan (1988). *Cry Hope: Positive Affirmations for Healthy Living*. Deerfield Beach, FL: Health Communications.

Vitale, Joe (2006). *Life's Missing Instruction Manual: The Guidebook You Should Have Been Given at Birth*. Hoboken, NJ: John Wiley & Sons.

Walls, Jeannette (2005). *The Glass Castle*. New York: Scribner.

Williamson, Marianne (1994). *Illuminata: Thoughts, Prayers and Rites of Passage*. New York: Random House.

Bibliography

Allen, Karen Neuman, and Danielle F. Wozniak. "The Language of Healing: Women's Voices in Healing and Recovering from Domestic Violence." *Social Work in Mental Health* 91 (2011): 37–55.

Bancroft, Lundy. *Why Does He Do That?: Inside the Minds of Angry and Controlling Men.* New York: Berkley, 2003.

Barnett, O., Cindy L. Miller-Perrin, and Robin D. Perrin. *Family Violence Across the Lifespan: An Introduction.* 3rd Ed. Thousand Oaks, CA: SAGE, 2011.

Carnes, Patrick. *A Gentle Path through the Twelve Steps.* Center City, MN: Hazelden, 2012.

de Becker, Gavin. *The Gift of Fear, Survival Signals that Protect Us from Violence.* Boston: Little Brown, 1997.

Engel, Beverly. *The Emotionally Abused Woman.* New York: Fawcett, 1990.

Grisby, N., and B. R. Hartman. "The Barriers Model: An Integrated Strategy for Intervening with Battered Woman." *Psychotherapy* 34 (1997): 484–97.

Hanson, Rick, and Richard Mendius. *Buddha's Brain: The Practical Neuroscience of Happiness, Love, and Wisdom.* Oakland, CA: New Harbinger, 2009.

"Is This Abuse?" Retrieved from *www. loveisrespect.org.*

Koepsell, J. K., M. A. Kernic, and V. L. Holt. "Factors That Influence Battered Women to Leave Their Abusive Relationships. *Violence and Victims* 21 (2006): 131–47.

Levine, Peter A. *Waking the Tiger: Healing Trauma: The Innate Capacity to Transform Overwhelming Experiences.* Berkeley, CA: North Atlantic, 1997.

Mark, Barbara, and Trudy Griswold. *Angelspeake: How to Talk with Your Angels.* New York: Simon & Schuster, 1995.

Tolman, R. The Development of a Measure of Psychological Maltreatment of Women by Their Male Partners." *Violence and Victims* 4 (1989): 159–78.

Turnbull, Colin. *The Forest People.* New York: Simon and Schuster, 1965

Walker, L. E. *The Battered Woman.* New York: Harper & Row, 1979.

Wozniak, D. "Rites of passage and healing efficacy: An ethnographic study of an intimate partner violence intervention." *Global Public Health: An International Journal for Research, Policy and Practice,* Volume 4, Issue 5 (2009): 453–63.

Wozniak, D., and K. Newman. "Ritual and performance in domestic violence healing: From survivor to thriver through a rites of passage intervention." *Journal of Culture Medicine and Psychiatry* (in press at time of this publication).

Index

About the Authors

Danielle F. Wozniak, MSW, ACSW, PhD, is both an anthropologist and a social worker and is an associate professor of social work at the University of Montana. Her research and passion have focused on women's identity, sexuality, domestic and sexual violence, and healing. Dr. Wozniak wrote the curriculum for the *Rites of Passage* groups for women healing from domestic violence and, together with Karen Allen, implemented them in three different states for women seeking to change their lives as well as training students and professionals. Her other books include *They're All My Children: Foster Mothering in America* and *Consuming Motherhood*.

Karen Allen, MSW, LCSW, PhD, is a professor and chair of the Social Work Program at Arkansas State University. As a social worker, Dr. Allen practiced for many years in health care, where as an emergency room social worker, she partnered domestic violence centers and the rape crisis centers in the area to improve care and services. Dr. Allen was part of the committee that worked to enforce mandated reporting laws in her state and also developed educational programs to promote awareness in health care providers about recognizing and intervening in situations where women were abused.

Please visit the authors at *www.survivingdomesticviolence.org*.